Quartet for J. Robert Oppenheimer

ALSO BY KELLY CHERRY

Poetry

The Life and Death of Poetry
The Retreats of Thought
Hazard and Prospect: New and Selected Poems
Rising Venus
Death and Transfiguration
God's Loud Hand
Natural Theology
Relativity: A Point of View
Lovers and Agnostics

Fiction

Twelve Women in a Country Called America
A Kind of Dream
The Woman Who
We Can Still Be Friends
The Society of Friends
My Life and Dr. Joyce Brothers
The Lost Traveller's Dream
In the Wink of an Eye
Augusta Played
Sick and Full of Burning

Nonfiction

Girl in a Library: On Women Writers and the Writing Life
History, Passion, Freedom, Death, and Hope: Prose about Poetry
Writing the World
The Exiled Heart: A Meditative Autobiography

Chapbooks/Limited Editions

Physics for Poets (poems)
Vectors: J. Robert Oppenheimer: The Years before the Bomb (poems)
The Globe and the Brain (an essay)
Welsh Table Talk (poems)
An Other Woman (a poem)
The Poem (an essay)
Time Out of Mind (poems)
Benjamin John (a poem)
Songs for a Soviet Composer (poems)
Conversion (a story)

Other

A Kelly Cherry Reader (stories, novel excerpts, essays, memoir, eight poems)

Translation

"Antigone," in *Sophocles, 2*
"Octavia," in *Seneca: The Tragedies, Volume II*

KELLY CHERRY

Quartet for J. Robert Oppenheimer

A POEM

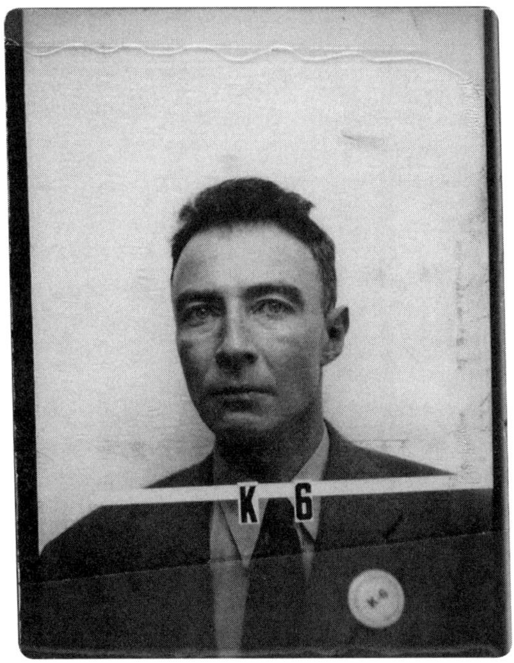

Louisiana State University Press
Baton Rouge

Published with the assistance of the Sea Cliff Fund

Published by Louisiana State University Press

Manufactured in the United States of America
First printing

Designer: Barbara Neely Bourgoyne
Typeface: Adobe Minion Pro
Printer and binder: McNaughton & Gunn, Inc.

Library of Congress Cataloging-in-Publication Data

Names: Cherry, Kelly, author.
Title: Quartet for J. Robert Oppenheimer : a poem / Kelly Cherry.
Description: Baton Rouge : Louisiana State University Press, [2017]
Identifiers: LCCN 2016027505| ISBN 978-0-8071-6504-1 (pbk. : alk. paper) | ISBN 978-0-8071-6505-8 (pdf) | ISBN 978-0-8071-6506-5 (epub) | ISBN 978-0-8071-6507-2 (mobi)
Classification: LCC PS3553.H357 A6 2017 | DDC 811/.54—dc23
LC record available at https://lccn.loc.gov/2016027505

The paper in this book meets the guidelines for permanence and durability of the Committee on Production Guidelines for Book Longevity of the Council on Library Resources. ♾

In memory of my brother, Mike Cherry,
who gave me my first Oppenheimer book

J. Robert Oppenheimer was a central figure of the twentieth century, which means that there are many different views of him. I have tried to be faithful to the figure as I see him after taking into account numerous, often conflicting, biographies, letters, reports, and reminiscences. Works I read (or viewed) *in toto* in the course of writing this poem are listed at the book's end.

CONTENTS

ACKNOWLEDGMENTS

I am grateful to the editors and staff who first published the following poems, sometimes in earlier versions: "Poetry in 1922" (*Atlanta Review);* "The Lacework of Coherence" (*Solstice: A Magazine of Diverse Voices);* "Dido Released to the Winds" (*Illuminations);* "White Sands" (*Shenandoah);* "Sonnet for a B-17" (*The James Dickey Review);* "Walking the Institute Woods" (*Vineyards*); "The Teahouse at Otowi Station" (*Arts & Letters*); "Pity Our Myths" (*December*); "Horses" (*Lake City Lights*); "The Great War" and "Two Preludes and a Bomb" (*Dan River Review);* "*Guernica*" (*Blue Fifth Notebook*); "Checkpoint Charlie (The Cold War)," (*Sin Fronteras*).

"Nights in the Secret City" and "An Idle Moment Some Days before the Trinity Test" appeared in *My Cruel Invention: A Contemporary Poetry Anthology,* ed. Bernadette Geyer.

"The Lacework of Coherence" also appeared in *SolLit: Solstice's Five-Year Anniversary Anthology.*

"Eniwetok, 1952," "August 6, 1945," and "Pikadon (Flash Bomb)" are forthcoming in *Nuclear Impact: Broken Atoms in Our Hands* from Shabda Press.

My gratitude wholeheartedly extends to Parallel Press of University of Wisconsin–Madison Libraries, which published, in 2012, my chapbook *Vectors: J. Robert Oppenheimer: The Years before the Bomb* in which the following poems appeared, sometimes in slightly different versions or with slightly different titles: "Introduction to Art," "The collection on the walls of the apartment on Riverside Drive," "At the New York Mineralogical Institute," "His childhood mineral collection," "Sundays," "The praiseworthy son," "Thanksgiving," "The Sadness in Him," "Outcast," "The Great War," "Sailing on Bay Shore, Long Island," "Discovering

New Mexico," "What Oppenheimer knew about composing poetry," "Poetry, Or the Special Theory of Relativity," "The Well-Stocked Mind," "The Poisoned Apple," "Robert the Dog," "Epiphany in Corsica," "Assistant Professor of Physics, University of California, Berkeley," "Oppenheimer, 1931," "The Wounded Warrior," "Scientists Flee Germany," "Aeneas and His Father," "Kristallnacht," "Hitler Redrawing the Map of Europe," "The Affair with Jean Tatlock," "Kitty," "The Women," and "Scientific Director of the Manhattan Project."

I wish also to thank the Los Alamos National Laboratories and emeritus archivist Roger Meade, the Rockefeller Foundation, and the Institute for Advanced Study in Princeton for gifts of time, archival guidance, and research assistance.

At IAS, Marcia Tucker, librarian, Christine Di Belli, archivist, and Erica Mosner, archival assistant, went out of their way to locate for me books, CDs, and Oppenheimer's professional correspondence. Christine and Erica cheered me on with my task, and I much appreciated that, the more so since I was working alone. Thanks also to Freeman Dyson of IAS for generously sharing his impressions of Oppenheimer and his wife. Peter Goddard, professor in the School of Natural Sciences (specializing in quantum field theory and string theory) and then-director of IAS, made it possible for me to be there as a Director's Visitor and showed me the office that had once been Oppenheimer's. His quiet kindness and professional manner made me feel welcome, and I am equally beholden to Lynn Staley, Harrington and Shirley Drake Professor of the Humanities and Medieval and Renaissance Studies at Colgate University, who suggested to him that my work would benefit if I could use their libraries. Peter Peret, professor emeritus in the School of Historical Studies, thoughtfully invited me to his house, which is the one to which Oppenheimer would have moved had he lived a little longer.

Poet William Jay Smith was a felicific source of encouragement as I worked on this book. I am doubly indebted to him for writing a recommendation to the Rockefeller Foundation.

I am also grateful to the Virginia Center for the Creative Arts for a Weinstein Residency during which I was able to complete the chapbook *Vectors: J. Robert Oppenheimer: The Years before the Bomb.*

My deepest thanks go to David R. Slavitt and Fred Chappell, masters of poetry, for their careful readings and shrewd notations.

Quartet for J. Robert Oppenheimer

INVOCATION

Invoke a muse? How quaint. But is it quaint,
considering that words appear upon
the page almost before one's thought of them,
or then again, retreat to sulk in sea-
side tents, refuse to come when called? Quaint

Muse,

allow a poet sentences with which
to praise a man, if not his killing weapons.
To praise his strength of mind. To his credit:
a war cut short, a world preserved, but gods—
who are tiny and numerous and interfering—
undid his fame and illness disassembled
his thoroughbred body, and yet his resonant name
bespeaks his deeds as one who earned the honor
due a hero: J. Robert Oppenheimer.

I. Vectors

1910–1911

Fleeing his wife, Leo Tolstoy dies
in a railroad station. Major Frank Woodbury
recognizes tincture of iodine
will disinfect the soldiers' impossible wounds.
Ernest Rutherford presents a theory
of the atom. *Atom azota* means "atom
of nitrogen" in Russian. Wheeler conceives
the idea of black holes, Matisse revels
in *Red Studio,* and the impetuous Kaiser
promotes his nation's "place in the sun." Everyone
tangoes.

Little Bobby Oppenheimer
settles in his mother's lap to nap.
It is a mystery, that he is other,
and what he dreams in his secure, snug doze.

EAST AND WEST

Hard-working German Jews on the Upper West Side
put distance between themselves and the *Ostjuden*,
who, they thought, were too Jewish, redolent
of shtetls and ghettos. They kept their Jewish traditions
and faith—a faith in their tribe if not in God—
while blending with successful Americans.
How was this wrong? They fancied their children growing
up in America, an American community,
with liberty and justice for all. But where
a few have more than others, enmity
grows like a bitter weed. Our local sun
does not shine on everyone. Envy
and resentment sink deep roots and strangle
the truth, as Oppenheimer was to learn
during the hearings. As for the present moment,
Oppie was ashamed of his self-made father—until
like Mark Twain, he discovered that the old guy
had somehow learned a helluva lot, and then
belated love for the father flourished in the son's heart.

INTRODUCTION TO ART

His mother may have been a bit distracted,
preoccupied with art, her painting much
more than a lady's hobby, the redbrick apartment
on Riverside a private gallery
for canvases by Vuillard and Vincent van Gogh,
Picasso, Derain, Renoir, and Maurice de Vlaminck.
There was a Rembrandt etching, a Cézanne drawing.
Gilt wallpaper shimmered in the shifting sun.
The boy drifted from room to room, sometimes
stopping to gaze at a work that caught his attention,
drew him forward: his mind expanded to
take in color, contrast, composition,
perspective, and the morning light that made
the pictures seem as if they'd just been painted,
if not by his mother, then by his own quick mind,
each brush stroke like a new idea, each
rich tone bright with meaning.

Obbligato. The collection on the walls of the apartment on Riverside Drive

Vuillard and van Gogh,
solar flares

among the dark furniture.

AT THE NEW YORK MINERALOGICAL INSTITUTE

At the age of twelve he gave a lecture on
geology to degreed geologists.
A little like Jesus discussing Yahweh
with learned elders of the synagogue.

—A false comparison, of course, given
the Oppenheimer family connection to
the School of Ethical Culture and its belief
in rationality and education,
its skepticism toward any theodicy
that would replace intelligence with dogma.

If there was a young Jesus, did he argue
that he himself was proof of God's existence
the way obsidian or basalt is proof
of volcanic activity?

Ostenato. His childhood mineral collection

Mica, sandstone, quartz. What fascinated
the curious child was light concealed inside,
the fugitive glint, the ticking heart of night.

SUNDAYS

Young Oppenheimer, raised among opulent,
elegant furnishings, was himself burnished
to a high degree of shine, educated
at the by-now-fabled High School of Ethical Culture.

On Sundays, in the Packard, their chauffeur
slowly drove the family along
the tree-lined street that hugged the Hudson River,
the boys' faces pale behind backseat windows.

Their mother masked her disfigured hand with a glove.
As days grew short and winter holidays
approached, the boys could smell chestnuts burning,
sense snow before it crystallized from air.

Their father pointed out notable details
of architecture. Ella corrected their posture,
her gloved hand no less firm for being gentle,
clouds of snow surrounding the Packard like

the sift of snow inside a paperweight,
how lightly but steadily it falls, how soon
the sky becomes invisible, the air
unbreathable, the glass globe suffocating.

ACCIACCATURA. THE PRAISEWORTHY SON

Can parents love their children more than children
can bear? Suppose a child is smart enough
to know he's not as brilliant or angelic
or handsome as they say. Does he not
feel profoundly the chasm between himself
and their praise? Their expectations? Even though
they say they have no expectations? A child
may fret and study all his life and still
believe it's not enough, it's never enough,
and when they try to tell him it is enough,
he smiles, says "Oh, okay," and goes away
believing that it's not, he's not and will
never be what they wanted him to be.

THANKSGIVING

Julius Oppenheimer loved his two boys.
Imagine him at dinner, head of the table,
feel his pleasure, his fatherly pride, perhaps
his surprise at finding himself impossibly blessed.
It makes him almost giddy, this bountiful harvest,
this cornucopia of bright children
whose intense curiosity and good manners
(they were taught to wear suits and ties to dinner)
welcome his homecoming day after day.

There was a third one, Lewis, meant to be
the middle one, dead after forty-five days,
a loss to which his wife would never be
reconciled.
                    Of course Bobby felt her despond
keenly, and doubted he could fill the shoes,
the baby shoes, that never would be worn.
We give ourselves to love before we know
our limitations, or those of our loves.

Miasma of sadness settled in, a fog
that lay, silent and quivering, a sleeping dog,
upon the floor and at the bottoms of beds.

THE SADNESS IN HIM

Always in him was the sadness of a boy
who felt unworthy of his parents' love.
As if he had to make up for the son
who died. As if he'd wished his baby brother
dead and then it happened. It didn't matter
that his parents loved him, or that his brother, Frank,
looked up to him nor did it matter that
he'd been too young to form a lasting memory
of the infant who died: he'd seen his mother tearful,
bereft, his father with his arm around her,
not speaking. Staring. Staring not at Renoir
or van Gogh or the small Derain or the Rembrandt etching
but at nothing. His parents' mutual heartbreak hushed
the apartment; he was afraid to play, even
by himself, afraid to make a noise, to draw
on a wall, to make a muddy footprint on
a floor or otherwise disturb their grief.
It wasn't their fault. Neither was it his.
So sadly much of sadness can be traced
to simple misinterpretation, and
it sets the mood for a lifetime.

OUTCAST

The other boys talked about it all
the time and he was curious about
almost everything. No surprise he wrote
his father to say that he was learning about
sex. He might have written his father to
brag that he was learning mathematics,
or how to tie and untie knots, or
construe Virgil, or memorize the Table
of Periodic Elements, but no—
these things, he already knew. Sex was new.

His father registered dissatisfaction
with the way the camp was run, and word got out.
Bobby became "Booby," "the tattletale,"
"the snitch." The daddy's boy who was too smart
for anybody's good. The kids ganged up,
stripped off his clothes, slapped green paint on his genitals,
locked him in an icehouse, and left him overnight.
He stayed awake until despair covered him
with dreams, makeshift rags for an outcast boy.

Lions chased him in his dreams, their paws
gigantic, the claws as huge and raking as backhoes.
Toward his father, whose wish to be protective
landed him here imprisoned and defenseless,
he felt anger, the taste of it metallic
in his mouth, but how does a son express anger
against the man who only wants the best
for him? So maybe he would die tonight,
maybe tomorrow all the boys would feel
ashamed, sorry, penitent, and dumb.

THE GREAT WAR

A single shot was fired, and all of Europe
reached for a gun. The poet Wilfred Owen,
twenty-five, devoutly Christian, confounded
by war's reality, determined his death
should be his protest against Absurdity
but near Amiens regretted his decision.
To die—perhaps to dream never again.
And yet, emboldened by the trust his troops
placed in him, he ran the deafening gamut
of automatic fire to seize the enemy's
machine gun and then turned the gun on Germans,
thus winning the admirable Military Cross.
To Siegfried Sassoon he wrote: "My senses are charred."
Yes; but he had soldierly duties and died
fulfilling them. The news reached his parents
as the bells of Shrewsbury sang of victory.

SAILING ON BAY SHORE, SOUTH LONG ISLAND

the air / the open air / the sky / the sea
their sailboat tacks / tacks again / again
and tips to starboard / turns nearly over / laughing
a pebble skimming the sea / the two brothers
alert / alive in their bodies / the sun / the sun
on their arms and shoulders / seaspray in their faces
no time to think of anything beyond
the lines / the mast / the boom / their young bodies
tense-taut / and stretched / the glittering sun on both
boys' backs and arms / the wind pushing / goading
the flashing wind / multifaceted sun
no time to think / only to be / to be

SUMMER BIRTHDAYS AT BAY SHORE

On summer birthdays—Ella's, Frank's—long scarves
of flowers gathered from the lawn and pieced
together signaled the house in Bay Shore festive,
but there was always laughter, Frank insisted;
excitement; pleasure doing, learning; and
guests who celebrated with the family,
plundering seven acres for scented blooms
to drape the table, chairs, and windowsills
yet even so the laughter struck the guests
as muted. Did the atmosphere reflect
the firstborn's lingering recondite depression?
Though the flowers' shout of color thrilled and cheered,
as did company and ritual, something
was awry with Robert, something he could not or
did not dare to name. The physicist Pais
would theorize that Oppenheimer was gay
even if he did not know he was,
and Sigmund Freud argued alcohol—
in which our boy indulged excessively—
was how the alcoholic defended himself
against his homosexual desires.
Now Pais and Freud are dead as dead letters
that went astray and wound up in a file
in an office in a building so obscure
no one remembers it beyond a few
diehard psychoanalysts who think,
unscientifically, that subconscious
motives/impulses can accurately be imputed
to all the acts that we perform. Thus Robert
loved the flowers that he cut, and loved
his mother, brother, and friends and finally
his father, "one of the most tolerant and human
of men," and when anxiety grabbed hold

of him and caused him to do rash or stupid
things, well, genius is not proof against
self-loathing or embarrassment or fear
of failure. Did he have what it would take
to be the paragon he thought his parents
wanted him to be, wanted himself to be,
great artist, architect or writer or scientist,
something, anyway, he could point to
and say *I did that, I made, discovered,*
wrought that one everlasting good, new thing,
brought to the world's party that birthday gift.

DISCOVERING NEW MEXICO

Seventeen. Sick, and stuck in his room.
It isn't difficult to recall the tumult
within the seventeen-year-old intelligence,
the lofty notions, ambition, pride compounded
with timidity and feelings of shameful failure.
A wonder it is that any of us survive
to rejoin the outer world—a world inhabited
not just by parents but by a seethe of life,
more life than had seemed possible inside
those four walls, that one preoccupied brain.
For a year, he lived on poetry and physics.
The next year, he consented to accompany
his English teacher Herbert Smith for a summer
in the Southwest. Camping out and horseback riding,
his spirits revived, his health improved. Away
from parents and invigorated by
the landscape, young Robert found a freedom
wider-winged than ever he'd imagined.
The colors of New Mexico were blue
and valiant yellow, sparked with moments of
green and rose (adobe rose). The sense
of space inspirits all who move within
that generous environment. Our Robert
experienced a new lightness, a new
energy. This ebullience encouraged him
to ask of Smith if he might take his last
name for his own and travel as Smith's brother.
Smith was shocked, aghast, appalled—though Robert,
perhaps, was merely caught up in excitement
and eager to express his gratitude
to and fondness for his much-loved teacher.
To be intense is sometimes to be thought
strange, simply because one does not know how to trim
one's feelings to the acceptable range of feeling.

STATIC ELECTRICITY

Reaching the mountaintop by horseback, the pair—
Robert and his friend Paul Horgan—rode
into a storm like the end of the world, rain
slamming their shoulders like a spray of bullets,
lightning bolts X-raying the darkening air.
They crouched beneath their mounts to eat their lunch.
Oranges for dessert. When Paul was done
with his, he gawped at Robert. Robert's hair
stood on end, strands in spokes sticking out
as if he were plugged into a live socket
or as if his mind were wired to infinity.

POETRY IN 1922

In 1922 T. S. Eliot
published *The Waste Land*, becoming Poetry King.

J. R. Oppenheimer made his own forays
into the field. *The field of poetry:*

a pale and deepening sky with newborn stars,
dew-damp grass, the owl in the cottonwood.

The field is wide and stretches out before
us for light-years. The field of poetry:

an ashen, sleep-deprived sky with ghost moon,
taffy-stretched shadows, the cataracted sun.

Con brio. What Oppenheimer Knew about Composing Poetry

The poet writing rides on a beam of light.

&

Grace note. Poetry, or the Theory of Special Relativity

You'll come back to a world you won't recognize.
You'll think that you've been gone barely an hour
but everybody you knew will have died of old age.
There will be a new party in power.

THE WELL-STOCKED MIND

The well-stocked mind's a pleasure to behold
(although the mind that lets itself be wrapped
in clouds and dreams may find a way to serve
some small, enduring purpose of its own).

At Harvard, Robert took ten—ten!—classes
each semester, then earned his Ph.D.
from Göttingen at twenty-two, wherefore
there are those who suggest that since his interests
were wide and scattered, he was without "focus,"
his precocious psyche "underintegrated."
Nonsense. He knew a lot and brought it to bear
on his understanding of this complex world.
If such a person is underintegrated,
perhaps the rest of us should loosen up,
allow a little light to come into
the room. Allow a little leeway in
the world.

PAUL DIRAC

> In science you want to say something that nobody knew before, in words which everyone can understand. In poetry you are bound to say . . . something that everybody knows already in words that nobody can understand.
>
> —Dirac to Oppenheimer (anecdote)

His good friend Paul Dirac, who may have had
Asperger's syndrome, had nonetheless a point,
but Oppie went on writing poems—which
he did not think were any good and yet
the writing of them brought him to a pitch
of creative excitement. If his friend didn't get it,
he did get it, and if his reader knew,
before reading, what Oppenheimer meant,
why that's the point of poetry, to bring
writer and reader into relationship
with truth and beauty, dear, dear Dirac.

THE POISONED APPLE

He considers the apple, the one in front of him,
an apple ripe with poison, lethal weapon
of his creation. No, he does not think
once of the vain stepmother in *Snow White.*
Nor could he think of Alan Turing, computer
pioneer and genius cryptographer, who
in thirty tech-savvy years will shed the world
like an outworn coat by eating half an apple
he has, it's thought, infused with cyanide.

This once, he does not think. He is transfixed.
He moves the apple from his desk to the desk
of his tutor Patrick Blackett. He is so envious
of Blackett that he wants him out of his way.
His head is full of unformed fantasies.
Cambridge rings his parents, who are visiting.
Julius pleads. Robert's put on probation,
shipped off to a Harley Street psychiatrist.
A close escape—for Robert Oppenheimer.

Or was the apple merely a metaphor,
as some suggest? A metaphor for what,
then? Ah, but no one knows, and furthermore,
it's as hard to believe a metaphor as an apple poisoned.

ROBERT THE DOG

A warm summer day in London. Harley Street.
Sitting among couples at a café, he ducked
beneath a table and began to bark.
"Dementia Praecox," said his analyst.
"Schizophrenia," we'd say today
yet surely what he suffered
was not that but anxiety, the disease
of smart people in their early years, when life
requires they recognize that they are still
apprentices and not yet in control
of anything—their work, their love (or loveless)
life, unknown and perhaps destined to be
eternally unknown, the knowing wished for
a simple competence acknowledged by
the masters of their trade. O youth, that is
so eager to collapse the time between
the present and the future—glowing future
in which one takes one's place among the masters
while throwing elegant and lively cocktail
parties on the patio with one's spouse beside one.
He'd have thought that he was playing a joke on his friend
Francis Fergusson. Well-dressed consumers of tea
or coffee or cognac stopped consuming tea
or coffee or cognac. Why did no one laugh?
He barked again and Fergusson came running.
The frozen crowd reclaimed its powers of
locomotion, moving politely away.
The hazy English sky seemed out of focus.

Apparently no one noticed that when he barked
it was because he wanted to be petted.

EPIPHANY IN CORSICA

On vacation in Corsica, something changed him.
A woman? Or Proust, who wrote of "that indifference
to the sufferings one causes, an indifference
which . . . is the terrible and permanent form
of cruelty."
                    If it was a woman
she must have been caring and kind, a woman in
whose hair he lost himself, the cloud of it
passing across his face as he kissed it.
This was a man bedeviled by demons
of his own creation. *Imperfect, imperfect,* they said,
those demons swarming around his ears like flies
or bees. If you have not had this experience,
enjoy your immunity to it. Robert
rolled groaning on the floor as if demented
and confirming the doctor's diagnosis, which
reflected the doctor's deeply wishful thinking
(no need to treat *this* obstreperous patient).

Far more likely is that Marcel Proust
awakened him from his waking, haunted sleep
wherein he was the central consciousness
of all that existed to a world he shared
with others and for which he bore a shared
responsibility.

ASSISTANT PROFESSOR OF PHYSICS, UNIVERSITY OF CALIFORNIA, BERKELEY

A blue-eyed hero,
tall as a god,
lean as Gary Cooper
or the young (but shorter) Richard Burton

some movie star anyway,
for sure

His students tried to *be* him,
his charisma was that intoxicating

They copied his walk,
his talk,
his habitual smoking

the way he held the chalk

they gawked at him,
mimicked his gestures

He loved being admired,
being liked, being
at the center. As if
he was the mind who made
it all go, the motor

in the machine.

OPPENHEIMER, 1931

His mother was dying.
Leukemia.

It was the Great Depression.
Grown men were crying

into their beer.
No one was buying

a house, a car, a coat.
"I am the loneliest man

in the world," he said to Smith,
his former high-school English teacher,

after his mother was dead.
I, he said.

Had he no thought
for his brother's pain,

his father's pain,
the grief of that old man

in the living room,
heavily sighing?

But loneliness is
a universe.

THE WOUNDED WARRIOR

"He worshiped her," said Smith.
                                        Into the pit,
now, the lethargy of unwillingness,
of refusing to try because he knows that what
he wants to happen can never happen—she will not
return and there is nothing left in life
to hope for. Days are smashed—they "lie in fragments."
Oppenheimer witnesses time's wreckage
but cannot repair what's broken. Nor can he speed
time up, as the still-fairly-young would like
to do. The pain of not yet being whole,
completed, formed, assails him as if he's
a wounded warrior, and yet who
is his enemy? Where is his sneaky rival?
What is the battle about and why, when he seeks
to counterattack, is no one there?

SCIENTISTS FLEE GERMANY

Scientists began to flee Germany,
fearing for their future. For two years
Robert dedicated a portion of
his salary to their aid. If his psyche
mirrored his anxious alliance with his parents—
his craving to escape the shame he felt
at their uncertain efforts to assimilate—
if he himself had fully assimilated—
he saw that his *gemütlich* life was absurd
compared with lives of Jews in Europe, where,
window by window, lights were going out.

GUERNICA

Picasso, oil on canvas, 1937.
A communiqué, a newspaper perhaps.
The beauty of the mural mandates close
attention to detail. It is not God
who's in *these* details (wounded horse, panicked
bull, dead child and mourning mother, bare bulb
of the interrogator's arsenal,
the severed arm, the bloody mess in black
and white and tacit red all over. Red
all over. Blood red. All over. All red).

AENEAS AND HIS FATHER

To my father, Anchises, I said: "Come, my father,
Climb up on my shoulders. You weigh so little.
Let us face together whatever happens.
My son shall walk beside me and my wife
Behind as usual. Now, my family,
Listen: Just outside the city, next
To a temple of Ceres and a mound, grows
A cypress worshiped by our ancestors,
And there we'll meet. Father, carry in your hands
The gods of our country, for I would not be guilty
Of sacrilege by touching them before
I wash off in a clean, running river
The blood and grime of battle."
                                                            I then threw
A golden lionskin around my shoulders
And bent to allow my father to climb on my back.
My son held my hand and kept up with us, even
Though he had to take two steps for every one
Of mine.

Thus did Aeneas bear Anchises on
His back, the weight less than that of his own son.

[*Aeneid* II, 11. 207–223]

KRISTALLNACHT

A darkening world. Bread lines in America
and Germany, and in the Soviet Union
the poets of an era exiled, shot,
disappeared. On people's faces, misery
and fear—if they dared to show their faces.
Most kept their heads down hoping to be not noticed.
They lived in tent cities or hired themselves
out like sharecroppers.
                                        Not everyone. Not
Robert Oppenheimer, who worked hard to give
his money away as grants for graduate students.
Still: paint this harsh decade dark and troubled,
with flames eating at the edges and
creeping toward the centers of the cities:
Berlin and Munich, Washington, D.C.,
Paris, London, Rome, Madrid, Vienna.

To blame somebody, to destroy competition
for food, land, money, to transfer their pain
and guilt—anti-Semitism served
such loathsome purposes. Who can forgive
us and the world we made?
                                        After the shattering,
silence. A silence not like the silence of death.
Rather, a silence like time holding its breath.
Shards lay on the pavement as if stemware
for thousands of Jewish weddings had been stamped on
by the black Fascist boot. History
was now married to horror.

HITLER REDRAWING THE MAP OF EUROPE

The failed painter Adolf Hitler redrew
the map of Europe. First Austria, and then,
Sudetenland and Czechoslovakia,
and with Stalin's help, Poland.
England declared
war against Germany. America
began arming, but *The Wizard of Oz* was on
the screen and Glenn Miller all the rage.
The children of that depressed age are called
the Silent Generation—earnest kids
who knew their parents had it rough, kids who
did not want to trouble their hurting parents further.
It came anyway, as we all know—trouble, war.
And still America dallied on the sidelines.
The days slid into one another while
the ailing Franklin Delano Roosevelt
awaited signs of more support for war.
Excitable American boys tossed
and turned at night in single beds in homes
where parents did their best to make sense of
the demanding future in which they found themselves.

Funebre. Postscript

And when the U.S. entered the war, our boys
were tough as nails hammered into coffins.

THE AFFAIR WITH JEAN TATLOCK

The pessimistic Jean, intelligent
and sad, drew up her stockings, pausing briefly
between, with one in hand, then straightening
the seams before she fastened rayon stockings
to garter belt. He watched the play of her hair,
its falling forward and backward, amber waves
of grain, had she not been a member of
the Communist Party. But who was not back then,
when anyone who wept on behalf of the poor
was suspect in the eyes of red-baiters?
She turned his attention outward toward the world
he'd seldom acknowledged since his first school days.
So long he'd been unaware and now—
amazed by the extent of his ignorance!
He'd wanted his life to turn in this direction
since reading Proust. Of course she was beautiful,
as was he in his manly way. Oh to be young,
with bodies limber and flexible, as tuned
as machines to their purposes. But Jean Tatlock,
easing the white slip down over her head,
her sinuous body, silk slip rippling tight
against her abdomen, released her heart
into his hands, which, trembling, let it fall.

KITTY

At last he married. I. I. Rabi, a colleague,
would one day say flat out that she was *evil.*
Evil? Unhappy, yes. Alcoholic,
yes. Ambitious and self-serving, but—
evil? She saw in Robert ambition equal
to her own and a way to fulfill it. He,
in his turn, saw himself magnified
in her eyes while she must have seen that he was one
of those dramatic men attracted to a desert
austerity, a T. E. Lawrence of physics.
(Great men are irresistibly sexy to
some women. The flashing in her eyes? Excitement,
which revved her pulse and warmed her skin all over.)
Even so, his own wishes were not
sufficient for him to take the proffered job.
What was *sufficient* was that Jews in Germany—
friends, colleagues, relatives, and scientists—
were daily in danger of savage crimes committed
everywhere Hitler's cockeyed and perverse
mania reached. Such suffering inflamed him.
In short, there was no way he could not accept.
Like Wilfred Owen, he believed in duty.
He didn't know that he was stepping off
a plank into a sea of fire, wherein
one could drown or be burned beyond recognition.

THE WOMEN

Jean abhorred hypocrisy, so crucial
to power; Kitty, widow and divorcée,
despised the people who despised the poor.
Neither woman would cede her politics
to her lover's. Both were rebels with causes, breaking
rules of propriety, whether in sex
or sympathy. The FBI might haunt
their homes, lean on neighbors for information;
the women were not intimidated. But
Jean was scared of demon shadows in her mind,
of falling from a cliff into a pit
of self-negation, and Kitty imagined that
when she gave birth, her child might swallow her
whole, like Jonah in the belly of the whale.

HAAKON CHEVALIER AND THE OPPENHEIMERS' FIRST CHILD

They parked the baby—Peter, nicknamed Pronto
by Oppie—with the Chevaliers and traipsed
off to Perro Caliente, the cabin in
New Mexico, until the start of the fall.
Their baby! Left behind as if superfluous!
But sometimes parents wait to fall in love
with babies and for now love nothing more
than what they love already—each the other;
their being in the world and advancing;
the work itself, the hint and tease of it,
the flash, the flare. At least the boy was safe
with Haakon and his wife. Kitty was glad
to be away; whereas Oppie worried.
But maybe not enough? What was he thinking?
That Kitty was too high-strung to be a mother?
That Kitty's nerves excused his own negligence?
His friendship with Haakon— Was Oppie, also, eager
for that last summer of freedom, and was it guilt
over his own complicity that, later, stopped
him from giving Haakon's name when so many
names were finally named? If a baby falls
in a forest, does anybody hear him cry?

LONDON

The winter skies of London: gray as ash,
and then they darkened as the Luftwaffe
flew over—aircraft knitting a dirty shroud
for the blanching sun. Each time the blitz began,
the Brits, great actors, put on a show of sangfroid
but were by no means foolish and dashed to safety.
Tiered bunks in shelters in the Tube stations;
canteen trains for the masses underground;
ticket queues; Blitz Scouts and the Home Guard
("Dad's Army"); the dank chill invading parlor
walls; blackened windows; sirens; bricks raining
from buildings; the country absence of the children:
another Troy? Perhaps. Or the only London
in the world.

LITTLE HOUSES

This little red house, the officer said, was built
for you. And you and you and you and you.
He checked them off, politely pointing to
the crematorium. A small white house
was added later to accommodate
the overflow that flowed and flowed and flowed
over the threshold. According to Rudolf Hoess,
Kommandant of Auschwitz, married mass murderer,
the doomed Jews walked "under the blossom-laden
fruit trees of the orchard." Bees dipped their legs
in pollen, and the pear trees' white blooms waved
in the last breeze of the day.

PEARL HARBOR

There are moments when our destinies change.
When Japanese fighter jets mowed down our ships and sailors
at Pearl Harbor, change was both personal
and worldwide. Destiny and history
collided. Cracks appeared across continents.
The fallout was huge. Colossal. More profound
than blind Homer's *Iliad* or Virgil's *Aeneid.*
Greater than Dante's punishing circles of hell.
Oppenheimer felt he might as well
be in one of those circles. Was it kosher
for him to feel responsible for so much?
Of course not. Then again, it was his job.
His duty. His project. His crew. His yoke. His tether.

Codetta. Some months later Robert Oppenheimer
became Coordinator of Rapid Rupture.
Things were rapidly rupturing all over.

SCIENTIFIC DIRECTOR OF THE MANHATTAN PROJECT

As in a drifting silence like the void
of outer space, young Robert moved among
eternal numbers kindled like the stars
with powers beyond the merely human—or
could heroic effort achieve such grand powers?
He came so close to singularities,
black holes, a theory of gravitational collapse,
but, in a characteristic hurry, set
this work aside. Did Robert understand
that he had forfeited the Nobel Prize?

Oppenheimer needed acclamation,
the actual life, the shine, more than more drifting
untethered through a void, through eager women,
through poetry, through alcohol, drifting.
A war was on, and he could be a leader
of men. Did he have even an inkling of
just what he was relinquishing? Or was
loss a given, as it was for most,
those stretched years of sacrifice and hardship.

Lives would be changed. The atom would reveal
a power incommensurate with its size.
The skies would open their doors, the firmament shift.
A man would find and lose and find himself.

II. Gadgetry

THE VIRTUOUS DEAD

Near by the withered tree, a dried-up well
leads down to another world, in which the shades
of precursor Greeks and Romans carry on,
though listlessly, attenuated lives.
How do they come to be so far from home?

So deep beneath the battle-scarred surface of
the earth, there are no nationalities.
Men so old their tongues are thick with dust,
the heroes of the classical past, remember
better times, swap war stories and tales
of athletic feats on well-groomed playing fields.

Aeneas, with Anchises on his back,
observed the fall of Troy. A great city
dying strangles on its people's cries.

ON NOT WRITING A CATALOGUE OF SHIPS

A catalogue of ships seems called for, what
with all those battleships and aircraft carriers
and airships, and the fishing boats that got
refugees and spies safely to Sweden
or were instrumental to successful sabotage,
and including the names of generals, heroes,
and commanders, but unlike the ancient Greeks
we harbor our history in history books,
which is why there is no catalogue herein,
but do not forget that loose lips sink ships.

TWO NOT OF A KIND

General Leslie Groves knew he'd found
his man, equipped with enormous erudition,
a theoretical thinker dedicated
to verifiable truth, a persuasive talker
able to elicit the allegiance of
mechanics, engineers, and physicists
toward a single aim: the atomic bomb.

The scientists disliked the strong-arm general
but the general didn't give a shit. Scientists
were needed, Oppenheimer needed, himself
the General needed, and that was all that mattered,
though promotion to Brigadier General
helped him to reach that contented conclusion.

As for Oppenheimer, he saw in Groves a guy
who'd support his scientific director and
whose tolerance for red tape barely exceeded
his own.
            The one a bulky ship against
the sky, the other a vanishingly thin contrail.

OPPENHEIMER AND THE DEAN OF ST. PAUL'S CATHEDRAL

Batter my heart, three person'd God. . . .
—John Donne

Tatlock introduced him to the poems of Donne,
that man of steely mind and passionate heart.
It was a meeting of like souls. He shared
Donne's penchant for yoking opposites
together, for seeing the sides of every problem,
for polarities that bend like Moebius strips,
and paradox that causes us to open
wider our always narrowly focused eyes.
As Oppenheimer loved the poems of Donne,
so Donne loved science, and as Donne loved science,
so Oppenheimer loved the poems of Donne.

Grace note. Solving equations on the blackboard

White stars in a black sky.

NEW MEXICO

The sky was wide open, a type of range
where roamed not antelope but a sun as orange
as pumpkins and white cloudlets like wild ponies.
Strings of sizzling red peppers against adobe
exterior walls reminded him of *mezuzahs,*
with their parchment prayers, nailed to doorposts in cases
often striking in their close-worked elegance,
though he was not observant, nor given to
religiosity beyond the usual
feelings of awe and oneness that attended
the scientific facts of his profession.
He liked the heady, horizontal space
of this place, which balanced the soaring ambition of
the reason he was here. The Sangre de Christo
mountains lifted and relieved his inward gaze,
resettled it upon the distant peaks.
The snap in the air caused his blue eyes to widen;
in them, a reflection of the galloping sky.

SOME SAY

That Hitler was compensating for having only one testicle.
That Hitler contracted syphilis from a Jew
and this was why he turned against the Jews.
That when his half-niece died he was broken-hearted
and crossed over into madness. That his madness
was genetically determined. That he compensated
for his failure as an artist by creating
an artistic design for genocide. Let us

say: hatred and envy riddled his heart and mind
like a disease, leaving vacant the places where
good sense and kindness might otherwise have lodged.

NEWSREEL

His wife was known to take a drink or two
or five or six with women friends as day
drove on toward pointless evening.
It's plausible that Oppie scorned their chatter.
Besides which, the day was deathly hot. Why not,
he thought, escape into an air-conditioned
movie theater?

                    In black-and-white,
the news precedes the film. He is face to face
with Jews behind barbed wire. It makes him sick.
He flees up the aisle to the men's room. Washes his face,
his hands, then dries them with a paper towel.
He wants nothing more than to drop the bomb
on Germany. He wants to blow Germany
off the fucking planet. He does not feel
less sick but at least no one can decipher
what has hit him. That is how he prefers
to be seen, or rather, not be seen. He is
a man of feeling afraid of feeling.

ON NOT WRITING THE HOLOCAUST

No poet who was not there can describe
the horror of the camps. We may recite
what we have read, or learned from videos,
but no one will be satisfied with a poem
by one who was not there. The poet may
describe the hellholes where people starved daylong
in darkness and isolation, the way they were treated
as worse than plague-ridden rats, the suffocating
smell of decayed or burnt flesh, but no one
will accept the poem as adequate. Therefore,
the poet concedes to historians and those
who *were* there—Primo Levi, Elie Wiesel—
the art of description, yet even so the poet bears
those images in her mind and they weigh
on her like ash and bone and cold, cold earth
thrown upon mass graves of the dead and still alive.

JEWS

The burnt. The starved. The buried alive.
Electrocution-by-fence. Experiments.
The snapped neck, the spinebroke back. The hanged.
Death by gas. Disease.
So many ways of killing the Jews.
Poison. Bayonet. Work
that made no one free. We can only bow our heads,
we who were not there. Should you meet
a Jew coming through the rye, shake his hand
for he has traveled far and into life
with stalwart heart and knowledge of the worst
humanity can do. Humanity?
Shouldn't we find another word for what
we are? This poem is open to suggestions.

LOS ALAMOS

The bridge by which the outer world could breach
the hidden city still is in place, a narrow
wooden-plank affair, as tenuous
as a hypothesis and yet triumphant,
though a newer bridge parallels the old.
For the site of Los Alamos, Oppenheimer
had chosen Pajarito Plateau, miles high
above sea level, volcanic mesa on which
a school was converted into the scientists' base camp.

The Project personnel now took it over.
They came on buses painted olive-drab,
the army's favorite color. The constant noise
of building drummed, heightening expectations,
like the soundtrack to a movie. Something big
was going on, and they would be a part
of it. The mystery and the magic of
their being there transformed them into soldiers,
allied with one another and alive
to the sun, the earth, the rocks and trees and air.

THE GADGET

His former student Robert Serber, now
a colleague, tasked with bringing up to speed
the scientists arriving in Los Alamos
almost daily, lisped perceptibly.
Even so, the lectures—on nuclear fission
—were a triumph, a brilliantly abbreviated
summation of what they knew at that point,
as clear and cogent as a syllogism.
The blackboard was on wheels and chalkdust flew
like snow, sawdust pouring from the ceiling.
Serber looked up. He saw a foot. The foot
had broken through the floor above. He went on
with his talk, but the outsider's foot, now inside the room,
reminded Oppenheimer of the need
for security. We know this, as he quickly
dispatched a different colleague to the front of the room
with a message to Serber, who, midspeech, began
referring to the "gadget," though he'd been calling it
the "bomb." What if the man with the foot through
the ceiling had been a spy? the scientists asked,
chuckling among themselves.

Twenty-five
years later, after Oppenheimer died,
Serber, now a widower, set out
with Kitty O. to sail around the world
in her fifty-two-foot ketch *The Moonraker*
that skimmed the silver light of Caribbean seas
but Kitty died at Panama Canal.
The man had loved all three: his wife, his boss,
his boss's wife. And science too, of course.
A scientist's love for science is intimate
and true.

THE NIGHT HE SPENT WITH TATLOCK AT HER APARTMENT IN SAN FRANCISCO

Depressed, and bisexual in America
when women in America could not own
openly their bisexuality,
Jean Tatlock called on Oppenheimer to
protect her from herself. He stayed the night.
J. Edgar Hoover thought *disloyalty*
and *lust, betrayal* and *unworthiness,*
though many men have stayed a night to talk
a woman out of death by pills or poison,
revolver, hanging, gas, or suffocation.
Despairing women ask that men embrace
them chastely, and sensitive men will do just that.
But Hoover, though a creep, had got it right,
and six months later Tatlock drowned herself.
Her father found her cold wet corpse.
                                                    Half
a year can hold a holiday, some books,
some favorable weather, birdsong, a child on a tricycle,
a good idea, and the joy of music. One hopes.

Adagio. There are those who think
a Russian working for the stars and stripes
arranged to have her murdered.
                                        Far-fetched, you say?
Maybe. Maybe not.

NIGHT

Full moon. And in a quadrant of the sky
Orion hunts, his dogs at heel. Venus,
lonely, shimmers in her satin nightgown.
Bodies like these make human bodies small,
eccentric things, playthings perhaps, like dolls
and Yo-yos. The human body is soft, unshelled.
Planetary bodies obey laws of
physics. After dark, in lighted rooms,
the scientists pushed one another to work
harder, harder. Piñion and juniper
sharpened the night air to a brilliant point.
The brilliant scientists sketched their brilliant thoughts
in quick equations on the blackboard, and
Oppenheimer approved, or squashed mistakes.
Outside, beneath the moon, an armadillo,
soft beneath its leathery armor, crossed streets
and gentle-hearted drivers braked.

DESPONDENCY

A friend found him slumped, with head in hands,
at his desk, clearly bone-tired and deeply despondent,
the substance of him frayed and verily shredded.
So still was he, he might have been a sculpture
by Giacometti called *Man Slumped at Desk.*
Light from the window slept on the desktop, like
a cat. Dust motes swam in the stream of light,
the bookmark in a book silent as a stone,
dropped paperclip dusty and unnoticed on the floor.
Imagine the look of consternation on
the face of his friend. Imagine the swarm of thoughts
in Robert's heavy head. Was it Tatlock,
his swooning, complicated Dido, who
despaired of justice, beauty, any hope
the world would heal from war's gravest wounds?
Was it the FBI, which spied on them,
voyeurs and tattletales, automatons
who have no understanding of emotion?
Was it the sick-making pressure of his job?
Or was it home life, private matters sealed
off from onlookers, those daily encounters and
confrontations that occur when no one's looking,
that spies don't realize are consequential
(although the phones at home and work were tapped)?
It seemed he'd never lift his head or rise,
a phoenix, from that sunbathed desk again.

Intimo. On the verge

He thought he wasn't suited to the job,
admitted to Bacher that he might resign.
But Bacher doubted his own ability.
Thus complaining, they encouraged each other.
It's good to have a friend.

THE TEAHOUSE AT OTOWI STATION

The chocolate cake was famously fabulous
but Edith, worried Tilano might imbibe,
banned liquor from her dinner table. "Los
Alamosers," as she called them, carpooled,
boozing before and after. A piñion fire,
fresh corn, a chicken wrung by the neck by her
or by Tilano, peas and squash and beans—
and raspberries on the chocolate cake, the cake
served with strong black coffee in pottery mugs.
On another day she wrote, *I saw a cloud*
pass over the earth on long grey stilts of rain.

DIDO RELEASED TO THE WINDS

At last omnipotent Juno, out of pity
For Dido's artless, shameless lovesickness,
Her physical pain, and her desire to join
Her husband in the afterworld, commissioned
Iris to deliver Dido from such suffering
Unto death, which was not possible
Until Proserpine received a lock
Of Dido's lovely hair. Then Iris flew
Down from Olympus on saffron wings bedewed
And refracting the thousand colors that compose
Sunlight and with her right hand cut the lock
From Dido's hair. "As I have been commissioned,
I give this lock to Dis, releasing you
From your body's agony." Therewith the warmth
Of that body fled into the wide world's winds
And Dido was cold, cold to the touch, and untouched.

[*Aeneid* IV, 11. 693–705]

DIDO IN THE FIELDS OF LAMENTATION

The Fields of Lamentation are the home
In death of persons love has misused and
Abused. Here they hide in glades of myrtle,
Grief clinging to them like their own shadows.
They wander, lost forever. Aeneas looks,
And there, among the others, is his Dido,
The Phoenician, her sword-wound fresh as a new rose.
Or so he thinks, in the twilight haze in which
Deer bound silently and mostly unseen.
Tears drenched his face as he spoke to her:
"Dido,
Dido, then the message is true and you are dead,
A suicide. Was it because of me?
Dear Queen, I swear I never would have left
You, never you, had not the gods willed it.
And it's because of them that I am here
Now, a visitor to this darkling realm
Where no bird sings and no one laughs. Dido,
I never meant to cause you such awful suffering.
Wait! Don't go! Are you afraid of me?
This is our last chance to speak together!"

And so he sought to calm her agitated
Shade, but Dido would not return his look,
Only stared at the ground. She was like a statue,
And then she was gone, having fled back to
The glades and groves, and the arms of her late husband,
Sychaeus. Had she heard a word of what
He said? She'd been so cold to him. And more:
Her fate seemed so unfair, and in his heart
He pitied her.

[*The Aeneid* VI, ll. 440–476]

NIGHTS IN THE SECRET CITY

Average age: 29. Bathtubs:
five. Lab alcohol: two-hundred proof
and though it mixes with water molecules
as soon as you open the bottle, it packs a punch.
Dorm dances, dinner parties, small flirtations
or wild improbable sexual liaisons.
The body wants what the body wants, and minds
alive with learning want what the body wants,
mind and body being a natural twosome.
A lot of fun was had. Feynman slapped
the bongo drums to exorcise the grief
he felt for his late beloved wife. Mountains
crammed with *los alamos*— "the cottonwoods"—
officiated like benign sentinels
undisturbed by human behavior. The sky, that sky
that stretches over the southwestern world,
like a god with a million eyes who lies awake
at night, may well have been somewhat amused.
The earth is small, its people smaller, and
tragedy perhaps merely a minor scene
in a much longer comedy.

THE OFFICE WIFE

A woman might drown herself in those blue eyes,
might rive her heart on his razor-sharp cheekbones
or immolate herself in his fevered mind.
Do I exaggerate? Ask Dorothy
McKibben, keeper of the gate—the entrance
to the secret city—and Oppenheimer's helpmate
in almost everything, even taking
his wife off his hands, or to Albuquerque.
It takes a woman to do that—devote
her life to a man who'd never belong to her.
But think of her importance to the project,
think how the days flew by like snowflakes caught
in a great flailing upward gust of wind.

OMAHA BEACH

The generals had done their math,
calculating X number of bodies
equal to one man alive for long
enough to get somewhere, for howsoever
short a time. And how long did it take
for troops to know that those first off the boats
were getting "slaughtered like hogs," someone said,
which meant stunned, eviscerated, cut, and deboned
or possibly just shot all to hell.
Some must have counted themselves fortunate
to survive with no arms or no legs or
only blinded by blood geysering from
the stomach wound only one guy over
or burned but only on one side of
his strip-mined, and exploded, cratered face.

The boys who did the fighting had to fight
not only Germans but their own unsayable fears,
their understanding that they were about
to die. Victory? It was victory
over more than the taking of a beach.
It was a terrible victory over the self.

SONNET FOR A B-17

The B-17 takes a hit in its third engine,
the propeller of which begins irrationally windmilling.
No nearby airstrip, and "too goddamn dark
to see the stars," the pilot says. He manages

to stay aloft for a couple of hundred miles,
losing altitude all the while, of course.
He reaches the Warsaw city park and crash
lands, taking out trees and shrubs. On all sides

young Polish soldiers materialize, rifles
aimed and cocked. Not one of the kids speaks English.
Just then, a Russian officer rides up
in a jeep and tells the boys to put down their rifles.

No one is hurt.
This is the kind of war story we like.

FDR / R.I.P.

Franklin Delano Roosevelt was dead.
All that night, snow fell in the Secret City.
The roofs of Bathtub Row—shrouded in white.

The town thought the world a carpet pulled
out from under them, the way a blizzard
whites out the horizon, vertigo taking hold.

Oppenheimer too had felt that spinning,
spinning out of control. His mouth was dry,
his hands on the shaky side of nervousness

as he stepped on stage. Offering consolation
to the inconsolable was not his strength.
They sat in rows in the movie theater,

waiting while he stood at the front and worried.
Well, he took a breath—a very deep breath—
and straightened his skinny-ass self to his six feet plus.

AN IDLE MOMENT SOME DAYS BEFORE THE TRINITY TEST

The low steady hum of fluorescent light,
the office deserted now except for one man
who wanders over to the open window,
listens to the locusts' soft shrilling
and looks up at the stars, which get top billing
in the desert night.

Capriccio. Porkpie

Oppenheimer's porkpie hat
kept the sun off his face
and made it easy for all to spot
the physicist in that top-secret place.

WHITE SANDS

A turquoise sky, its overflowing light
splashing down on buttes, mesas, mountains,
ravines, arroyos, canyons, caves, and flats,
white sands where scaffolding abuts the sun
and engineers are measuring the space
between annihilation and the view.
Oppie's porkpie hat shadows his face.
(A skinny rabbit wisely leaps out of his way.)
He's nervous, tense, afraid that something will
go wrong—there is so much that even now
can go wrong. There is the question of fallout.
He hugs himself while smoking, arms crossed,
a pose so characteristic, so often noted,
that actors who play him do the same. The flood
of light is only a metaphor, of course.
In general, deserts are dry, and men
measuring white sands are a mirage.

DESERT FLOWERS

All those men roaming the southwest desert—
soldiers with machine guns plugging antelope,
engineers building bunkers and a crate,
scientists in a state approaching hysteria,
and all of them, all of them, taking leaks.
It is a wonder the desert didn't stink,
that ocotillo and yucca managed to survive.
(The urine must have dried immediately.)
When Oppenheimer strolled off for a discreet piss,
he strolled back with a debonair air and a desert flower
in hand to offer to whoever was there.

Fröhlich. Life in desert country

They choked on dust, and scorpions turned up
in their beds. They worked an eighteen-hour day
in 100-degree temperatures.
There were accidents, mistakes, and practical jokes.
A good time was had by all.

THE STORM

The towering shot tower treacherous with run-off
from the storm, cable banging in the wind,
ice picks of lightning slashing the bold-faced sky
and one poor guy to guard the site against
sabotage though no saboteurs turned up
that night, thank heavens. Thank too the thoroughly soaked
single guard. Around the tower's base:
mattresses, in case the gadget fell,
or a scientist. The cable kept on clanging.
Oppenheimer couldn't sleep. General
Groves slept like a well-fed, overlarge baby.
I. I. Rabi showed up in a black homburg,
umbrella in hand, and when the storm moved off
the sky grew clear as the clearest of complexions,
suffused with dawning pink.

EMILY DICKINSON AT TRINITY

the flash
the mushroom cloud
the loud devouring roar

zero at the bone
fire at the core

TRINITY

A thunderstorm wracked their scaffolding on the night
before the test. It might have been bad luck,
it might have been the anger of the gods,
but then the weather cleared as dawn approached,
crawling from the cave of unremembered time
like a child attempting first steps.
Trinity
was the name Oppenheimer gave to the site,
perhaps in tribute to Tatlock or Donne or
the *Bhagavad Gita.* Or all of those.
The time was five thirty a.m. Only
Oppenheimer wore a coat; it was
July. He also wore a suit, the suit
now baggy, the man's body emaciated.
He also wore his porkpie hat. He leaned
into a post. Wiped his face. "Lord,"
he said, "these affairs are hard on the heart."
His old bête noir, anxiety, clouded
his face until "it was lit by reflections from
the sand," says Abraham Pais, of what
some saw as Oppenheimer's triumphant glow
that monumental day.

TONGUES OF FLAME

Cross the river
Go down through fire
The hero's mother burns
on the eternal pyre

Odysseus was in hell,
seeing his mother's shade

brighter than a thousand suns
they said, after the blast
after the conquering future
became the uncorrectable past

Who shall be saved?
Already, the tongues of flame
lick the backs of his hands,
saying his name

TRINITITE

Nearsighted, you might at first think grass has grown
at Trinity Site, the desert a lawn, the lawn
a lunch for Nebuchadnezzar. These bits of green
are trinitite, sand alchemized to glass
by bomb blast. Or say *a sea-change rich*
and strange. What Oppenheimer knew before
the bomb was not what he knew afterward—
truth too easily forgot. *Between*
the idea and the reality falls
the shadow of a doubt, as Eliot
might have written—should have written, if
he'd been honest with himself. The present poet
shores these fragments against her crumbling heart.
We can't put back what physics rips apart.

TWO PRELUDES AND A BOMB

On Sugar Loaf Hill on Okinawa
the mud in which American soldiers slipped
and fell face first was rich with maggots and feces.
Twelve thousand Marines died in that fucked-up muck.

A Japanese submarine torpedoed
the USS *Indianapolis,* which sank
in twelve minutes. Four days and five nights,
with no food, no water, American sailors struggled
to escape the sharks that picked them off and dragged
them down through black water. Out of their minds,
they were, imagining the Officers' Quarters—
and drinkable water—lay on the bottom of
the ocean.

                August 6, the *Enola Gay*
delivered Little Boy to Hiroshima.
If any kind of God existed, surely
he would have been ashamed to show his face,
which means there was no God around that day
though there were people trying to help people
and maybe people like that are a kind of God
or church. Tsutomu Yamaguchi, a man
of business, burned by the bomb in Hiroshima,
traveled home to Nagasaki just in time
to be irradiated by the bomb
code named Fat Man.

AUGUST 6, 1945

The boy perched on the steps.
The day was as clear as the child's eyes,
a day made for perching on steps.

After the bomb, the boy is gone—
not fishing, not to school, not
called by family or playmate,

just gone, his shadow burnt
into those stone steps,
himself mere air.

At the same moment,
language comes to an end.

We cannot speak, our voices crack
and break, our tongues stumble
through the ruins of the tower of Babel.

PIKADON (FLASH BOMB)

The blast boiled flesh from bone,
ground bone to grit, flake, and shard.

What more is there to say?

White light in silence,
the moment suspended—
a woman changed to air—

What more is there to say?

Like a dog with a bone
winds shook the city.

What more is there to say?

A man carried his eyes in his cupped hands,
palms open, as though his hands might see
what he could not.

The still living
envied the dead.

What more is there to say?

Black rain fell.
What more?

The sickness began.

AFTERWARD

He said to Truman, "Mr. President,
I feel I have blood on my hands." From that,
we know that first he asked himself, *Did I
cause this?* Was he a murderer? A killer
of children? "We have known sin," he also said.
If anyone has sinned, retorted Bridgeman,
it's God, by making fission possible.
Meanwhile, Truman was having none of it.
The blood, said Truman, was on his *presidential*
hands, and he was not the sniveling showoff
Oppie was. What Oppenheimer could not
say was that he meant *My poor daughter,*
and *poor daughter* stood for all the children
in this fallen world that he had changed and that
he could not change back.

THE NATURE OF WAR

Of course he had blood on his hands. Who did not?
Everyone did, including pacifists,
who let others do the killing. It is the nature
of war to spill like a river over banks
into the ground on which we walk, infecting
every one of us with sin. Is *sin*
too theological a word? Say *crime,*
as in *crimes against humanity.* A war
anywhere seeps into our hearts, our veins
flushed with worrisome discomfiture and remorse.
A good war, we say, and we are profoundly grateful
to those who won it. And yet—

Grace note. Kyōchikutō

At last oleanders bloomed in Hiroshima.
The Japanese took heart. If oleander
could survive, Hiroshima could survive.

PITY OUR MYTHS

> Pity our myths. . . .
>
> —Oppenheimer, as quoted by David Lilienthal

Pity our myths, for they are few and frail
and tear like Christmas paper, sputter out
like Sabbath candles. What we think we know,
we know not. The blue-eyed Buddha escaped
earth's sorrow by achieving enlightenment
but where does that leave us? Sending troops
overseas—Pacific, Atlantic, Caspian—
wherever blood is spilled, wherever it flows
in the firmament. The beautiful classical gods
age badly, splendid talents gone to seed,
their once-fabulous lives reduced to routine.
And the myths of the North, of a race of mighty men
and strong women with gold-spun hair and rings
that gleam in musky moonlight, who tells them now,
and who would want to, knowing where they lead?
Poor myths indeed, worn to bare bone, clacking
the same old same old, while yet the scientists
are telling us of new discoveries,
the strangest tales of all, narratives of
materials, measurement, gravity, and mind.

WAR

Like Aeneas, like Achilles,
quite like the warrior-kings of old,
a leader calls together strategists
and makers of arms and bearers of arms.
Thus did Oppenheimer, not in revenge
or excess but to save civilization
from the brute mindlessness of Fascism.
Can anyone think that Oppenheimer was *not*
shocked by what he'd done? That he was un-
perturbed by all the dead, the obliterated, the burned,
the maimed, the scarred, the sick, the suffering,
the irradiated, the deformed, the mourning
of Hiroshima and Nagasaki? He was human.
His wife clasped his hand.
She stroked his head.
She waited for his coughing fit to stop
and steadied him. A melting blaze slid down
the west to rise in the land of the rising sun.
We know that war perpetuates itself,
that cruelty has lasting consequences,
but we don't know anything that he didn't know.
Life finds us between a rock and if not
a very hard place then an empty place,
abyss, black hole, the void, or Avernus
where Persephone withdrew to winter with Hades.
We learn to live without assurances.

III. Kangaroo

I. THE NATIONAL MOOD

Not without reason, the national mood turned sour,
and much more sour than was reasonable.
Reasonable men like George Kennan advised
a policy of "containment" to keep at bay
the alien and, thought some, satanic
political system of Communism, contagious
as it seemed to be. An Iron Curtain divided
humanity into opposing species,
and so began the Cold War that threatened
to turn hot, hotter, hottest. Unreasonable men
like Joe McCarthy looked for Reds beneath
beds, and in Hollywood moguls strangled
themselves twisting to conform, blacklisting
screenwriters who dared to write for the down and out.
There is no brief to make for the Hitlers and
the Stalins of the world but government
in general leans toward corruption like
the friend of a friend claiming to be a friend.

II. THE "VISTA" REPORT

When Oppie cut a person down to size
blood was drawn. Strauss, whose ignorance Oppie
demonstrated to him, neither forgave nor forgot
while Edward Teller, feeling put upon
by Oppie, believed the director denigrated
the "super" he'd designed. Thus enemies,
enraged and powerful, multiplied.
The clash of egos!—thrust and counterthrust.
A sword fight, and we all know what "swords" are.
The Air Force fumed and railed when Oppenheimer,
in his report, suggested Western Europe
would be better off using tactical bombs
instead of bombs that would blow the world to hell.
Besides, Alger Hiss and Klaus Fuchs were spies,
the reasoning went; why not Oppenheimer,
who'd made no secret of his leftist leanings?
Double besides, the man was *not* a saint.
The CIA knew all there was to know.

III. TATLOCK REDUX

Or so They thought, but wiretaps, photographs,
and keeping tabs on Tatlock and Oppenheimer
(all illegal activities), left Them
in the dark when it came to Jean's sexuality.
She hesitated to marry Oppenheimer
because her shrink informed her that she was
a lesbian, at least to some degree.
They knew she suffered from depression, but
did They know, or care, that her lauded father was
an anti-Semite? And for that matter, did
They know if They Themselves were anti-Semites?
Jean was angry, sad, and stuck, and lacking
a women's movement that might have saved her. She
who hates herself requires a savior, being
unable to reclaim herself from darkness,
the baleful clouds, black as blindness, that blocked
from view her born freedom, the spacious skies
and shining seas of her American birthright.

IV. THE FIFTIES

It was the Fifties. Men were men. Women,
despite a few exceptions that "proved" the rule,
adjuncts. A first-class stamp sold for three cents.
Director of the Institute in Princeton
since 1947, with an office
in Fuld, the building bibbed by a swag of green,
and brilliant colleagues such as Albert Einstein
with whom to walk and talk and smoke and joke,
Oppie relished his position. Chairman
of the General Advisory Commission,
adviser to the President, and holder
of a "Q" security clearance, not to mention
his status as a true American hero,
how could he have anticipated his fall,
that swift, disastrous, plummeting, great decline?
The last year of the Forties, Soviets tested
their own atomic bomb in Kazakhstan,
with help from spies in the States. The arms race was on.

V. ENIWETOK, 1952

Elugelab, an island off the atoll
of Eniwetok, disappeared forever
when scientists set off a hydrogen bomb.
A fireball like a gigantic fear-blanched face
stretched its mouth and swallowed the horizon.
It changed the sea to red, incarnadine
as well-water turned to wine in Canaan,
but the sea was not effluence of pressed grapes
nor a miracle performed by Jesus Christ.
The island itself blushed red; burned for six hours.
Elugelab was gone. When Teller heard
the test was a success, he telegraphed
Los Alamos: "It's a boy." (Original
his mind might be, but he clung to societal convention.)
Upshot? We'd lost our opportunity
to coax the Soviets to the table, where
both sides would forswear hydrogen bombs.
The H-bomb—flagrant harbinger of Doomsday.

VI. TRAPPED

> . . . wisdom itself cannot flourish, nor even truth be determined, without the give and take of debate or criticism.
>
> —Oppenheimer to Eleanor Roosevelt on *Round Table* show, February 12, 1950.

He lost his cool—an affect never more
than surface-deep. Was flustered and confused,
rabbit-twitchy. *I was an idiot,*
he said, unraveling. He should have listened
to Einstein, who told him not to go
or go and tell the panel where to go.
The letter said that if he did *not* go,
he was admitting guilt. He went to clear
his name and named names, seeking to establish
his bona fides. A noose was growing tighter
around his neck; he panicked. Outsmarted, then,
by the vain and vengeful Strauss who didn't blink
at breaking the laws, tapping the phones of Oppie's
legal team, withholding documents from the same.
It didn't stop there. Strauss did his best to chase
him out of the Institute. *Schadenfreude,*
one has to call it. A word that sounds beautiful
but stinks like roadkill, a skunk in the drainage ditch.

VII. MACHIAVELLIAN

> . . . I have now served for some twelve
> years. . . . If I were thus unworthy I could
> hardly have served our country as I have
> tried. . .
>
> —J. Robert Oppenheimer, Letter to Lewis Strauss

And more skulduggery behind the scenes:
J. Edgar Hoover, like Lewis Strauss, had cleared
the physicist in 1943,
but now they charged him yet again—of what
they'd cleared him of! Tapping his lawyers' phones,
they knew the lawyers' plans *before* the hearing.
The chief charge: that Oppie obstructed progress
on the H-bomb despite the Bravo test on Bikini
Atoll a bare few months ago that scared
the pants off the President and wrecked the habitat
for years to come, the islanders left *sans* fish.
A synonym for *thermonuclear:*
megadeath. And that of course was why
Oppenheimer was against it. Teller
somehow convinced himself the bomb he built
would wipe the Commies out of Hungary
(his home) while not affecting anyone else.
Even great minds are subject to wishful thinking.

VIII. ROOM 2022

Asked if he had been approached by spies, Oppenheimer named George Eltenton, saying G. E. had approached three scientists, of which he was but one. Later he admitted he'd been approached only by his friend Haakon Chevalier, whose approach was on behalf of George Eltenton. He was trying to protect his old friend Chevalier. During the hearing he was not allowed to refresh his memory with transcripts of previous interrogations.

An inconspicuous building in D.C.
(the better to keep proceedings under wraps).
Room 2022, a disused office
making do as a rudimentary courthouse.
Defense was shown a basement room in which
to work at night, a room bugged and ramshackle.
Upstairs, Oppie, shown to a beat-up couch,
waited with the sun in his eyes (equivalent
to an interrogator's overhead bulb).
Aware the hearing itself endangered security,
to his own disadvantage he stayed silent
about anything classified. The lie he'd told
eleven years before to keep his friend
Haakon out of trouble was now a gun
at his head. His shirt slick with sweat under the arms,
Oppenheimer fought to control his fury,
his fear, his feeling that he was a mouse
being toyed with not by cats but dreamsprung lions.

IX. AFTERSHOCK

His enemies should have known that E. M. Forster
hoped, between his country and his friend,
to choose his friend. Which Oppenheimer did.

*

I. I. Rabi told them Oppie served
his country brilliantly. He even declared
the hearing absurd. For after all, Oppie
was a consultant. Nobody *has* to consult
a consultant, so what was the point of holding a hearing?
But Rabi also thought Oppenheimer
caved to his enemies, that he lacked grit,
hadn't a sufficient amount of emotional strength.
Perhaps he was once more the miserable boy
locked inside the icehouse, stubborn enough
to stay the night but sad and wondering
why the kids mistreated him. Was he so bad?
Kitty suffered too. Escorting friends
to their car after dinner, he heard her wail
as if someone, or something, suddenly had died.

X. HENRY SMYTH

A serious fellow and loyal citizen,
Henry Smyth, who had no knowledge of
Strauss's shenanigans, nevertheless
could see a witch hunt when he saw a witch hunt.
Despite a promise otherwise, a vote
was taken whether to release the transcript.
To this, Smyth wrote the one dissenting opinion,
on which he worked for weeks. His wife, Mary,
kept a diary, tracking illicit maneuvers
in the hearing, noting also the toll it took
on her husband, who barely slept or ate, determined
to do all he could to avoid a travesty,
and though he wasn't Oppenheimer's friend,
he was a friend *to* Oppenheimer, and
the benevolent unseen angel at the table.
Or rather, there were two truth-loving angels
at that table, dinner dishes pushed aside,
the Stilton and a pear left on a plate.

XI. WHAT THE GODS DO, WHAT THE GODS DID

The gods, who are tiny and numerous and interfering,
dislike hubris and always punish it,
but not to teach a thing or two to mortals
and not because their aims are loftier.
The gods are jealous of man, that passionate creature
whose time is short and therefore purposeful.
Observing Oppenheimer's giddying success,
the pleasure he took in being instrumental
to science and sound government, they sought
to bring him down: to hurl him off the peak
of the mountain and cast him into disregard.
Into the Princeton house subdued by shame
crept shadows of depression. Kitty's drinking
took over. The children were tentative, their father
bearing a bone-deep, heart-deep sense of failure.
Truer to say his country failed its servant.
If tears appeared in those blue eyes, they were tears
for what we all had lost—a safer world.

XII. THE WORLD'S A PLACE

A "farce," he called it later, and it was.
A tragedy, too, for him and for America.
A chemistry professor Strauss appointed
to the "court" and thought was in his pocket as
a hard-liner refused to play by Strauss
and Teller's handbook. Ward Evans made it clear
he thought the hearing would be an unriddable,
shameful stain on this country's history.
Sometimes people have good sense and courage.
But Edward Teller's testimony plunged
a knife in Robert Oppenheimer's back.
And what mistakes are being made today
regarding crime and punishment and public
safety? At any given moment so
many vectors are in play that none of us
can know or guess the outcome. The world's a place
where crosswinds blow and wrangle and a snow-
fall dazzles on the darkest night of the year.

IV. Actual Philosophy

> Theoretical physics is actual philosophy.
>
> —MAX BORN

HERO'S RETURN

Seeing Aeneas has the golden bough,
Charon ferries the Sibyl and her companion
Across the River Styx.
                                        Aeneas joins
Deceased Anchises, and the son and father
Together tour Elysium, the fields
Of shades, the breeze-wicked plain of fallen heroes.
Anchises, with the foresight of the dead,
Speaks to Aeneas of wars he's destined to fight,
Explains the people of the Laurentin
And Latinus, the city, and how to deal
With both. There are, he says, two gates of sleep:
A one of horn for dreamy shades true blue,
A harder one of polished ivory
Through which the Gods of the Dead funnel false dreams

Aboveground. Anchises takes his son and the Sibyl
To the gate of gleaming ivory. But why?
Because they are not shades? Because the world
We know is false? Is packed full of false dreams,
hallucinatory and misleading dreams?
Aeneas seeks out his ships, meets up with friends.
They coast along the shore to Caietas harbor.
They throw the anchors from the prows. The sterns
Rest on the shore.
                                        "Remember," says Anchises,
"By your power you are required to rule the nations
Wisely, to bless the peace with law, to spare
The conquered and caution those who would go too far."

[from *Aeneid* VI]

ORPHEUS

Oppenheimer foresaw the Soviet regime
acquiring duplicated plans from spies
as happened with the atomic bomb. In this,
he was savvier than Edward Teller. For this,
his enemies set upon him like a pack of reiving wolves
or ravening Maenads who tore Orpheus apart,
the pieces of his body carried out
to sea, the deep salt sea that drowned his song.

THE KING OF POETRY VISITS THE INSTITUTE

Cunard from England to America,
arriving in October, breezes brisk,
leaves in reds and yellows like football teams
assembled on a playing field.
                                        Sixty,
his wife deceased in an insane asylum,
he seemed to his scientific colleagues snobbish,
disdainful. Never did they dream the King
of Poetry could be intimidated
by foreign languages of math and physics,
the clouds of chalk dust emanating from
the chalkboards in their offices, scrawled
with formulae and symbols.
                                        What had he
but the objective correlative, some poems,
some essays, notes for a play. Aha! In his office,
he, too, had a chalkboard. One day he chalked
a kind of diagram of his play in progress,
assigning to his unnamed characters
Greek letters: alpha, beta, gamma. Just
like the physicists! He allowed the board to stand
unerased as long as he was there.
Which wasn't long. Stockholm awaited him:
the Nobel Prize in Literature.
                                        It seems
The Waste Land was what nudged Oppenheimer
to study Sanskrit. *Shantih shantih shantih:*
the peace that passeth understanding. And
if a poet writes a poem and no one reads it,
does anyone hear the poet, falling in
a forest?

THE PUEBLOS' OPPENHEIMER

From pueblos in San Ildefonso to
the city on the hill trekked workers who
washed and dried and swept and cleaned and shined,
who wove and mended, cooked and straightened, who
took care of children and bestowed sweet treats
upon them, workers who suspected some-
thing was afoot but knew not what till later.
When *Life* put Oppenheimer on the cover—
the photo by the famous Alfred Eisenstaedt—
these workers hung the picture on their walls
beside their portraits of the holy saints.
Did Oppie hear of this? Maybe not
and maybe it was better if he did not,
for he'd probably have thought that to be prayed
to meant he should be better than he was
and he had blamed himself for that for years
already.

FAME IN AMERICA

In America fame is a double-edged sword.
It dubs you important and then cuts you down.
Your head rolls off the horseshoe table where
the judges sit who have already formed
their judgments, two of the judges in collusion,
withholding evidence, case carefully stacked
against you. People envy famous people,
and your sundered head is being kicked around
like a football. The football is beat up and battered
now, and somehow you have to reattach
the thing to your neck. Go on as if nothing of note
has taken place. Pretend you are not dead,
are alive and whole. This is what fame does
in America: vanishes as if it never was.

MATURING

Of many forms anxiety can take,
sententiousness may be the most annoying
as words fall from the open mouth to land
painfully upon the listener's head
rather like a dreary rain of marbles
or nanobombs, compact and nonexploding.
In short, pomposity will alienate.
Poor Oppie thought he sowed his pearls of wisdom
but yet his listeners, exasperated,
had found his careful language dense and slick.
Good thing he finally grew confident
enough to shed his preachy pretensions and
feel at ease in his very sensitive skin.

ANXIOUS PEOPLE

Anxious people long for answers and if
the answers aren't forthcoming will supply
their own. Thus Oppenheimer interrupted
his fellow physicists and sometimes smirked
or grew agitated when someone took too long
to grasp the point. So eager are the anxious
to make sure all is right, they gum up the works,
make a mess of everything. That is no way
to put one's friends—or enemies—at ease.

Now cancer took its toll. No longer in
a race against the passage of time—he knew
that time had won—he worked as hard as always
but abandoned extracurricular haste and showy
postures, and was free to be himself—
the self not harried or harrowed, the self itself.

PROCESS OF ELIMINATION

Definitely not schizophrenic.
Not bipolar.
Not paranoid.
Not a psychopath.
Not OCD.
Not a narcissist.
Subject to depression but solved it with work and a schedule.
Could be hypermanic, flying high on work or play, but who can't?
Depression and hypermania often accompany anxiety.
Anxiety can drive you out of your mind for a while.
Anxiety was the cause of his strange breaks from reality,
as a process of elimination makes clear.

MERMAIDS

> There is a real, positive record. . . . What more do you want, mermaids?
> —I. I. Rabi, defending Oppenheimer at the hearing in 1954

Mermaids rocked the boat,
fishtails flipping fore and aft.
The mermaids swam and sang,
making waves.

Fishtails flipping fore and aft,
singing was heard on the shore.
Making waves,
a wind from the west bullied the sea.

Singing was heard on the shore,
echoed in coves in the cliffs.
A wind from the west bullied the sea,
messing the mermaids' hair.

Echoed in coves in the cliffs,
the mermaids' song grew loud as archery and ax.
The mermaids' mussed and flowing locks
entangled the mermaids' swanlike necks.

The mermaids' song grew loud as a storm,
sending a renegade boat to wreck on rocks,
the mermaids' swanlike necks pinched and strangling.
The moon drowned in the sea.

A renegade boat wrecked on rocks.
Beware, beware of mischievous mermaids
maddened by the sinking moon
for they'll rock your boat mercilessly.

HORSES

At Perro Caliente, the horse was named Crisis.
A perfect name, since Robert thrived on crisis.
He loved the rush of adrenaline through his body
and courted that surge with too-fast cars, twisty
boats on turbulent waters, the dangerous freedom
promoted by the buzz of alcohol,
telephone calls from men in high places,
and women who believed they needed him.

But now, at Princeton, he and Kitty rode
two horses: Topper and Step-up, names sedate
as Queen Anne chairs. Sunlight spread out its skirt,
picnicking on the lawn, and when it dipped
below the horizon, a drift of cirrus clouds
glowed as if the skies were radioactive.

WALKING THE INSTITUTE WOODS

Beyond the trestle tracks there is a path
that calls the dream-besotted soul to rest.
Nothing hurries here. There is no clock
that chimes, and time is neither running away
from him nor running out—not yet—and now,
just now, the earth beneath his steps a greenhouse
for beech trees, aspen, maples, oak, and dogwood
will not quake or otherwise give way.
How grand the trees in their abiding grace,
uncompromising in devotion to
his late-day walk, their fidelity
to peace.

THE LACEWORK OF COHERENCE

We know so little but the little we know
we place beside a neighboring bit or byte
of information, thereby shaping knowledge
as fields of knowledge, finding correspondence
or at least links among the fertile fields
or, as Robert Oppenheimer poetically said,
"a kind of lacework of coherence." Lace-
work, lovely as it is, is full of holes,
or maybe one should say *scattered abysses,*
drop-offs into darkest incomprehension
or maybe one should say *our state of knowledge*
is raddled with abscesses, burnt-up cells, the windy
emptiness of old, failed, dejected men.
But now, let's think of lace as something like
a constellation of stars, emphatic stars
cohering in an image of mysterious beauty,
Orion with his hunting dogs, the twin
brothers of Gemini arm in arm.

OPPENHEIMER AND THE *BHAGAVAD GITA*

Whereas Christians fetishize suffering,
the Hindu recommends self-abnegation,

eclipsing the ego, darkness on the sun—
were that not wrongly suggestive, hinting at

something sinister while what is wanted
is freedom, a certain kind of freedom from

the self and all its selfishness; therefore,
concomitant anxieties; therefore,

a subjugation of the will to power.
A quiet heart. Still soul. No fear of loss.

But this is hard for the Westerner to do.
One may relinquish all, as saints have done,

but Westerners dislike passivity.
Whatever peace of mind Oppenheimer

found, he found by losing himself in work
and books and art and friends and music, not

nirvana, moksha, shanti, paradise.

PRÉCIS OF THE LECTURE "THE OPEN MIND," FIRST DELIVERED BY J. ROBERT OPPENHEIMER IN NOVEMBER 1954

The artist and the scientist alike
must live in loneliness, the scientist
because a wider audience is not
attuned to symbols and the statements that
she proffers in regard to what she does.

Meanwhile the artist hasn't a common myth,
experience, or sensibility
to draw upon, nothing to unify
an audience or connect his orphic work
to it or to the languishing (because

fatigued, eclectic, changed, and out of sorts)
"great, open, windy world." But creativity
"is a proper charge on the university,
and the university a proper home for" him
as it is also for the scientist.

Thus universities, as patrons of art
and science, help; and art and science must
speak to each other.

ON *SCIENCE AND THE COMMON UNDERSTANDING* BY J. ROBERT OPPENHEIMER (THE REITH LECTURES, BBC, 1953)

One thinks of C. S. Peirce, philosopher
who wrote about the scientific method,
the role of error in the search for truth,
and the elemental categories of
firstness, secondness, thirdness. Oppenheimer
refers to Peirce in a piece on Einstein,
from which we guess at an acquaintance with
the extraordinary mind of the man whose work
anticipated his own *Science and*
the Common Understanding. One likes to think
that Oppenheimer thus derived the sense
of a shared tradition, an understanding that
he himself was not a lone mad dog
baying at the cheesy moon.

SMOKING IN BED

Since Oppenheimer smoked a plurality
of cigarette packs per day, say four or five,
it's not surprising that he smoked in bed.
But Kitty also smoked in bed, and nightcaps
for both were de rigueur. Oh, hell—we might
as well call them lushes, codependents, birds
of an alcoholic feather. Kitty burned
a multitude of black holes in the sheets,
so unhappy she half-wanted to burn
the house down with her and Oppie in it.
Who can assuage an emptiness like that?
Not that she did not try, tending her garden,
her exquisite garden, to perfection, but
one needs a purpose, even a depressed drunk.
Or rather, especially a depressed drunk.

The furniture ticked in the hollow silence of
the night. In her mind she saw the pillows go
up in a shower of flames, her torso charcoaled,
her nightgown melting on her wilted breasts.

DRINKING

Somewhere along the line she would have screamed
I hate you.
He would have locked his face
against hers. From her hand,
he would have eased the martini glass
before she could throw it, whether at him or the van Gogh
he'd inherited from his father, *Enclosed Field*
with Rising Sun, that hung on the bright white living room
wall in Manor House. She would have cried.
He would have consoled her.
He would have cried later, or half-cried, or at least almost cried.
She'd have left, gone out into her sweet-scented flower garden
restrained by four rock walls, gazed at the stars so far away
they made her dizzy. She would have lain down on the grass
and slipped from the stream of consciousness.
The alchemy of dew and moonlight worked upon the silent lawn
a shivery change to silver.
A night owl called.
A diligent spider spun a thread through her tangled hair.

EXPERIMENTAL SYLLOGISMS

The country of which he is a citizen calls on him.
They ask him to do a job.
Because he is a citizen he does what he is asked.

He considered his job a duty.
He did what he was asked to do.
Therefore, it was done.

When it was done, he rejoiced in the accomplishment—
for about a minute.
Fungus in the sky;
therefore, the world upside-down or inside out.

As numbers of the dead came in from Japan,
he sickened. He recoiled.
Therefore, he felt he had "blood on his hands."

But he couldn't change what was done. He did not disown his work.
He could only argue against it.
Therefore, he did.

Therefore, he asked the country of which he was a citizen
to take sensible steps to keep the nation—the world—safe.
Therefore, his country said he was no longer needed.

He bore the humiliation with dignity
but he was sick, a sick man walking,
a man too sick to walk. Therefore he died.

The horrors of a single day on earth are beyond counting.
Joy is found in the interstices.
Therefore, seize not the day but the interstices.

RECEIVING THE FERMI PRIZE

The morning of that day in Dallas, Kennedy
called Oppenheimer on the phone to say
that he'd be getting this year's Fermi medal.
It would be, perhaps, a sort of apology
from America to the man who'd tried so hard
to save us from ourselves after the war,
only to be thrown onto the side of the road
like the butt of a cigarette or empty carton
of Chinese takeout. A few hours later Oswald,
from a window in the Texas School Book Depository,
blew out Kennedy's brains with a bolt-action rifle.
Jackie was left holding them in her hands.

The country was in shock. No one knew
a season of assassinations had begun.
When December came, it was Lyndon Johnson
who read the citation to Oppenheimer. Oppie
was frail by then, fragile as stemware. He'd shrunk,
and his eyes had sunk Delphic-deep in their sockets.
Those eyes were simultaneously gratified,
bemused, mirthful, cynical, and bitter,
all of which surely were appropriate
to the occasion.

Impetuoso. Fermi's fingertip

Enrico Fermi lost a finger's
tip to clumsiness in a lab.
He picked it up, brushed it off,
and tried to feed it to his cat.
The cat turned up its nose. Who knows
if Fermi's cat was as smart
as Shrödinger's?

CHECKPOINT CHARLIE (THE COLD WAR)

Searchlights interrogated frozen ground,
small islands of snow, the twisted barbed wire designed
to rip the shirt from the back of a desperate man,
his skin from his broken leg. What a war that was,
with spies who wanted in from the cold, lovers
and families separated by functionaries
who cared not a whit for love or family,
dogs barking in a no-man's-land, sirens
that screamed the terrifying scream that meant
the would-be escapee had been caught or shot
or would be shot (there was a shortage of options
for those who wished to travel west). Remember
the desolate barricade, the frigid air,
the smell of danger everywhere.

A YELLOW HOUSE ON ST. JOHN, HAWKSNEST BAY

He swapped the desert for a sapphire sea,
a broad beach white as gesso and as smooth
as satin sheets (thanks to coral reefs),
bay rum and starfruit smelling of cinnamon
where puffsoft sand gave way to scraggly shrub.

They promised not to rent the house to others
but did. Promised to return the property
but did not. Bananaquits (called "sugar birds")
chittered in the trees and on the veranda.
Beneath blue skies, our hero mixed martinis.

The sea was calm or rough and Oppie sailed
whatever way it was. Sunlight played
the waves like a piano. Such transactions are
"the ceaseless transformation of energy,"
to steal a phrase. Or they are among them.

The mongoose and the dragonfly reside
on St. John—not exclusively, of course.
Humans? Certainly fewer then than now.
Which was what he liked about the island:
The privacy. Freedom from prying eyes.

THE LATE CHANGES

Dying, he shrugged off remaining mannerisms,
forwent his pride, which had, on occasion,
sustained him through rough times. The time for masks
was gone. Far less given now to elision—
the hidden steps that led to his remarks—
he was humble, straightforward, soft-spoken still, and stoic,
doing his work despite the pain that barked
at his body. What is a body anyway?
A house for dream and memory, the third
roommate being sensory awareness of
the present. The ring of the telephone, a whiff
of wisteria so potent one imagines
that one can taste it, the feel of fresh linen
or draft of soft air, the ever-new view
of sunrise over an enclosed field.

DEATH OF A HERO

Throat cancer. The eternal pipe,
an infinite series of cigarettes.
He underwent radiation.
Gone, the doctors said, but no:
limousines from Princeton to cobalt
in New York City. Kitty asked
Freeman Dyson to talk physics
to her husband but Dyson held his hand
in silence. At the start of the year,
1966, Robert
weighed 100 pounds and stood six feet
tall but had begun to stoop,
the beautiful blue eyes now stones
at the bottom of wells. He thought of writing
a book about "the history of
recent physics." He saw his daughter
graduate from Oberlin;
but his voice rasped like cans dragged
across a street. He made it to
the APS meeting in Berkeley.
After dinner, Serber walked
him and Kitty to their car.
At the last minute, Robert said
the cancer was back.

It spread first to
his palate, then his tongue and then
his Eustachian tube.

Kitty pleaded
with her husband's secretary to find
a gun in case the cancer traveled
to his brain. Robert intervened,
escorted her—his secretary—
to the door, and said to her, "I hope
that one day you will see this, too,
as a joke." *Vide* Beethoven's
"The comedy is over." Robert
begged a friend to "look after Toni
in the future." It was January
of the new year, the last faculty
meeting looming on the calendar.
Preparing for the meeting, Robert
studied all the applications,
knew all the candidates' names and knew
also that he would not live to meet
the people he was recommending.
His voice was gone, flown from his throat
to someplace where words can rest easy,
as in an easy chair or hammock,
and Robert himself went home to bed.

He fell into deep sleep, and deeper
sleep still, the brilliant brain turning
down the lights, hard-used lungs
slowing, *the battered heart* grinding
to a halt—but so carefully,
with such reticence,
that no one knew just when he died.

THE MEMORIAL: ADAGIO AND ALLEGRO FROM BEETHOVEN'S QUARTET IN C SHARP MINOR, OPUS 131

The tributes first, and a tape of *Dies Irae*
by Stravinsky—Balanchine's selection—
followed by the music he chose himself:
a late string quartet by Beethoven,
adagio gravely lovely, a reckoning,
allegro electric with energy, both leading
to, originally, the Grosse Fuge,
in which Beethoven climbs to heaven on a ladder
woven of strings to knock on God's closed door
and have it out with him, man to man.

NOT SAINTS BUT HEROES

Men are not saints but sometimes they are heroes.
It happens when they are inspired to act.
Inspired, as in "a spirit enters in."
Enters in, as in "to fill the lungs
or heart or mind, indeed the man entire."
Entire, as in the case of a physicist
who lent his energy and passion to
the effort, desperate and drastic, to
invent a weapon that would win the war.
A few of Oppenheimer's physicist pals
accused him of a lack of focus, of
a weakness for the arts and literature
as if a string quartet is not as hard
and clear as diamond and as if a poem
is not as packed with meaning as an equation.
Yet all agree that only he could bring
them all together, like an orchestra.

(A woman, too, can be a hero, and
like men, women are not saints.)

HEROES HAVE FLAWS

Heroes have flaws and those flaws are always fatal.
That's how the tiny, interfering gods
do what they do—they find or make the flaws
and advertise them. Or are they merely stagehands
drawing a curtain? But no. They play on human
weakness. Consequently Oppenheimer,
who might have known enough to know better,
fell for his image in the mirror, where
he mixed with powerful people, chaired or sat
committees, navigated corridors
knowing where they led as well as he knew
the Periodic Table. Essential to
decisions, called upon by major players
in the press, the government, the military,
the universities—who could rebuff
such sweet seduction? Not the naïve boy
who'd been humiliated at camp, young man
who collapsed into insanity although
only for minutes at a time, husband
whose wife demanded to be married to
a special man, significant man, man
regarded by his peers as more than a peer.
And wasn't he that man?
                                        But break a law
or bend the truth or fudge an answer to
a question, and tiny, interfering gods
usurp one's conscience.

TO OPPENHEIMER, ON HIS DAUGHTER

A daughter is a delicate, whimsical thing,
no matter she's a tomboy. First she's on
her back in her crib, gumming the black right ear
of her much-loved toy panda, big as she.
The morning light spills in from opened windows,
a wave that breaks against the modest pink
of her young unpainted lips, the mystery of
her cool, glistening eyes. She learns to read
and write and already she has moved into
her own unknowable world, which does not, cannot
adjoin your tangled, frayed, and fallen world,
your worn-out boring world. She soon displays
a talent for sailing off the warm coast of St. Croix.
She goes to Oberlin to study languages,
French, Italian, Spanish, German, Russian
and she's picked up Creole English on your trips
to the Virgin Islands. She can do a perfect
West Indian accent.
After Kitty gives
your ashes to the Caribbean Sea,
your daughter tries to drown herself in just
that spot. She misses you and thinks it would
be lovely living underwater with
her dad forever. She is beautiful
but timid as a ghost, with long dark hair,
a princess, if princesses only had
long dark hair. She marries and divorces,
then marries and divorces a second time.
Applies to the United Nations to be
a translator. She's qualified, for sure,
but they have to run a security check. They go
through *your* files and deny her clearance.
That
hurt. She felt she had been buried alive,

had no life of her own, had only a half-life,
like uranium, and since it made a kind
of sense she killed herself though not by drowning.
Instead, she hanged herself. Just thirty-two.
In the yellow house you built and Kitty later
willed to her. On that island with bananaquits.

WHY HE RECITED POETRY

Some thought he willfully obscured his meaning.
The metaphysical poets! *Bhagavad Gita!*
Such high-flying rhetoric, a fondness
for ambiguity and the mandarin.

Some thought fine language worked a spell on him—
a kind of spell—tricking him into daydream
or wool-gathering, leading him astray.
Why else would he have drifted so far away

from hard physics? Why else? This is why:
he was too private to strip his feelings bare
but poetry, philosophy, and Proust
perfectly expressed his tongue-tied feelings.

Some thought that he was coy. Coy, or
oracular. It wasn't so. He went
to books to find himself. A reading man
discovers truth in beauty and finds freedom

in diamond-hard carefully faceted lines
of poetry. To understand him, one
had only to read what he had read. One had
merely to discover the truth in word-wrapt beauty.

Grace Note. Complex freight

A letter Robert wrote at twenty-four,
to his brother, argues that a poem expresses
itself and only itself, not commentary,
not manifesto, neither truth nor error,
and that indeed was Modernism, but poems
are built with words, and words emit meaning,
and often enough, meanings plural. And then
and there is where the fun begins. Error
and truth vie with poets for supremacy,
though poets often are oblivious
to this while working, for metaphor and tale
conspire to overcome their better sense.
A poet loves the complex freight of meaning,
its brilliance, subterranean turns, radiant
heat and artful music. If he dares
to write a poem that manages to be
more than itself, someone may complain
but what is that to one who swears by meaning?
Meaningless.

OPPENHEIMER'S SON

Peter lost his father, mother, sister.
He may have felt the family was cursed,
if not by gods, by some craziness
carried in the genes, some lethal bent
of mind or mood, some dark proclivity
for the dark. Father, mother, sister,
in that order.
                        He escaped, and since
escape is epic in its consequences,
may kinder gods attend him where he goes
and silence the tenacious, murmuring shadows.

BEATING THE DEAD HORSE

The FBI still checks on Oppenheimer
nearly half a century after his death.
They seem to hope he's turned up at the Institute
as hard-driving as ever, a tailored ghost
in the blue Cadillac convertible
turning into Lot A beside Fuld Hall,
the Admin building in which his office was located,
where he could look out toward a field and trees.
Has someone checked to see the wiretaps are gone?
Maybe by now the quondam agents who tailed
the physicist are ghosts themselves. Maybe
the ghosts of agents who shadowed him are spying
still in Hades, though from afar, as surely
the likes of them are not allowed to trespass
in Elysian Fields. Maybe Robert dwells
in those far fields and wears a crown of laurels,
and maybe he and Homer take turns reciting
the travels and travails of sly Odysseus,
the wily one. With Plato he discusses
the ideal state, its nature and its purposes.
Dammit, he said, teary-eyed, *I happen*
to love this country.
America, he meant.
Frazzled and sick, and finally dead, and still
they will not leave him alone. Shhh. They see
him now with Dido. They get out their cameras.

NO MORE NUKES

Prompts for the end of civilization include
global warming, methane gas, and tides
usurping coasts. Pandemic contagions also
will do, or possibly an avian flu,
and asteroids abound; an asteroid
could knock us off our orbit. Still, the bombs
we've built, the "A" and "H," hold us hostage
as no natural catastrophe can do,
because we *choose* to live this close to doom.
Not simply death but *doom:* the death of all
the works of man. J. Robert Oppenheimer
wished that he could put the genie back
into the bottle and, allowed to come back
to life and take apart all assembled,
stockpiled bombs wherever, would with glee
and satisfaction do exactly that,
but we must do it for him, and our world.

IT'S NOT TOO LATE TO CLEAR HIS NAME

What's wrong with us, that we cannot be bothered
to honor the honorable dead

Americans: we hasten toward the future
as if the past is something used,
a sprung couch carried to the curb
a rug a dog peed on

But if we stop, we hear a billion voices,
each a call for justice. Cannot we right
one injustice among the billion?

Do we think that by honoring one man we dishonor others?
But we know that clearing his name will make no difference
to him. It *will* make a difference for our country.

To correct an error is to cleanse the soul.

OPPENHEIMER THE MAN

Not many men were called to lead their troops
of scientists in war against Fascists
in Europe and Japan. One called thus
was Robert Oppenheimer. Not many men
undo the knots they've tied themselves into
but Oppenheimer did. Not every man
survives the scripted smearing of his good name
and carries quietly on with his job while life
drains from his spirit like oil from a failing engine.
Not every man will honor his marriage vows
to a wife turned dour and drunk and querulous.
And most of all, not every man attempts
to wake a nation drugged to nightmare sleep
by right-wing hysteria and government greed.
Oppenheimer did.
                    The pampered boy
afraid to break the decorous silence in
his parents' Manhattan apartment with all the art
addressed the world, concerned for all of it,
and tried to tell us that civility—
international civility—
is the vital cornerstone of civilization.
And who will disagree with that? None but
the uncivilized.

MAN

> As for man, his days are as grass: as a flower of the field, so he flourisheth. For the wind passeth over it, and it is gone; and the place thereof shall know it no more.
>
> —Psalm 103:15–16, KJV

Man is nothing, not even grass.
Say, a straw in the wind.
Say, a leaf on a path
but that is already too much.
A path suggests direction, progress.

A straw in the wind
or in the beak of a bird
fashioning a nest.
On Omaha Beach men disembarked
and died almost instantly.
Straws in the wind.

Man is nothing, not even grass
or a straw in the wind
or a leaf on an overgrown path.
His friends die,
his name is forgotten.
Where are the Etruscans, the Minoans, the Christian martyrs of the young Roman Empire?

Man comes into existence and goes out from existence.
The time of his life lasts a nanosecond.
What is man? Nothing.
Not even grass. Not even an ice cube
in a glass of water.

He makes a stir, perhaps—a fuss, an agitation, a small commotion,
his actions measured by their effect on others
but otherwise invisible,
the feeblest of breezes flirting with winter-killed grass.

ASHES AND STARDUST

> *Stardust* is a scientific term referring to refractory dust grains that condensed from cooling ejected gases from individual presolar stars and mixed into the cloud from which the Solar System condensed.

Ashes and stardust we are,
nothing more, nothing less.
Our passions and learning—evanescent,
here and then nowhere. Not there. Not there.

Perhaps this person's thoughts may be found in a book,
that person's dreams in a work of art,
someone else's discovery or invention in a laboratory
or classroom. But where are all the others?
Here and then nowhere. Not there. Not there.

And the love between lovers? The love of a parent
for a child? The child's love for a teacher?
The love anyone had for someone?
There is no love in death, nor any I.
We are here and then nowhere. Not there. Not there.

Earth to earth. Dust to dust.
Presolar stuff to presolar stuff.
The director says, *It's a wrap!*
And it is.
We are here and then nowhere. Not there. Not there.

WORKS CONSULTED

Auden, W. H., and Christopher Isherwood. *The Ascent of F-6*. London: Faber & Faber Ltd., 1936. A play.

Bacher, Robert F. *Robert Oppenheimer 1904–1967*. J. Robert Oppenheimer Memorial Committee: Los Alamos, New Mexico, 1999. Rptd. from *Proceedings of the American Philosophical Society*, Vol. 116, No. 4, August 1972.

Barnstone, Tony. *Tongue of War: From Pearl Harbor to Nagasaki*. Foreword by B. H. Fairchild. With an introduction and notes on the poems. Kansas City, MO: BkMk Press, 2009. Poems.

Bethe, Hans A., Henry De Wolf Smyth, and George Kennan. *Three Tributes to J. Robert Oppenheimer*. Princeton, NJ: Institute for Advanced Study, 1967. Program.

Brandon, Ivan. "Husband Says Suicide Victim Depressed." AP. *The Virgin Islands Daily News*, January 24, 1977, p. 5.

Bernstein, Jeremy. *Oppenheimer: Portrait of an Enigma*. Chicago: Ivan R. Dee, 2004.

Bird, Kai, and Martin J. Sherwin. *American Prometheus: The Triumph and Tragedy of J. Robert Oppenheimer*. New York: Knopf, 2005.

Blackwell, Jon. "Security Risk." *The Trentonian*. www.capitalcentury.com/1953.html.

Born, Max. *My Life and My Views*. Intro. by I. Bernard Cohen. New York: Charles Scribner's Sons, 1968.

Breit, Harvey. "An Interview with T. S. Eliot—and Excerpts from His Birthday Book." *The New York Times*, November 21, 1948.

Broad, William J. "Transcripts Kept Secret for 60 Years Bolster Defense of Oppenheimer's Loyalty." *The New York Times*, October 12, 2014.

Brode, Bernice. *Tales of Los Alamos: Life on the Mesa 1943–1945*. Preface by Barbara Storms, ed. Los Alamos, NM: Los Alamos Historical Society, 1997, 2006.

Buruma, Ian. *Year Zero: A History of 1945*. New York: The Penguin Press, 2013.

Canaday, John. "Critical Assembly." Poems about assembling the A-bomb. Pieces published in various magazines. Selections available at www.atlengthmag.com. In progress.

Carr, Alan B. *The Forgotten Physicist: Robert F. Bacher, 1905–2004*. Los Alamos, NM: Los Alamos Historical Society (Monograph 6), 2008.

Cassidy, David C. *J. Robert Oppenheimer and the American Century*. Baltimore: Johns Hopkins University Press, 2009.

Church, Peggy Pond. *The House at Otowi Bridge: The Story of Edith Warner and Los Alamos*. Albuquerque: The University of New Mexico Press, 1959.

Conant, Jennet. *109 East Palace: Robert Oppenheimer and the Secret City of Los Alamos*. New York: Simon & Schuster, 2005.

Curie, Eve. *Madame Curie*. New York: Doubleday, Doran, 1937.

Day One. Produced and directed by David W. Rintels, based on the book *Day One: Before Hiroshima* by Joseph Sargent. Acorn Media. Color. Actors: Brian Dennehy, David Strathairn. 140 minutes. DVD Release Date: November 13, 2007.

Doctor Atomic, opera, music by John Adams, dir. by Peter Sellars, DVDs recorded at the Netherlands Opera, June 2007. Premiere, San Francisco Opera, October, 2005. Metropolitan production, October 2008.

Dyson, Freeman. *Disturbing the Universe*. New York: Harper & Row, 1979.

———. *Weapons and Hope*. New York: HarperCollins, 1984.

Feynman, Richard P. *"Surely You're Joking, Mr. Feynman!": Adventures of a Curious Character* As told to Ralph Leighton. Ed. by Edward Hutchings. New York: W. W. Norton, 1985.

Fehner, Terrence R., and F. G. Gosling. "The Manhattan Project." April, 2012. www.energy.gov/sites/prod/files/The%20Manhattan%20Project.pdf.

———. "Unlocking the Mysteries of the J. Robert Oppenheimer Transcript." www.energy.gov/articles/unlocking-mysteries-j-robert-oppenheimer-transcript.

Flenniken, Kathleen. *Plume*. Seattle: University of Washington Press, 2012. Poems about the Hanford Nuclear Reservation.

Frayn, Michael. *Copenhagen*. New York: Anchor Books, 2000. With Postscript. A play about Niels Bohr and Werner Heisenberg.

Garner, Dwight. "After Atom Bombs' Shock, The Real Horrors Began Unfolding." *The New York Times*, January 19, 2010. A review of *The Last Train from Hiroshima* by Charles Pellegrino. New York: Henry Holt, 2010.

Goodchild, Peter. *J. Robert Oppenheimer: Shatterer of Worlds*. Boston: Houghton Mifflin Co., 1981.

Hartshorne, Charles, and Paul Weiss, eds. *Collected Papers of Charles Sanders Peirce*. Cambridge: Belknap Press of Harvard University Press, 1960. Eight volumes.

Hersey, John. *Hiroshima*. A new edition with a final chapter written forty years after the explosion. New York: Vintage Books, 1989.

J. Robert Oppenheimer Personnel Hearings Transcripts. Vols. IIa, IIb, VIa, VIIa, IXa, IXb. www.osti.gov/opennet/hearing.jsp.

Jenkins, Edith A. *Against a Field Sinister: Memoirs and Stories.* San Francisco: City Lights Books, 1991.

Kanon, Joseph. *Los Alamos.* New York: Island Books/Dell, 1997. Novel.

Kelly, Cynthia C. *Oppenheimer and the Manhattan Project: Insights into J. Robert Oppenheimer,* "Father of the Atomic Bomb." Singapore: World Scientific Publishing Company, Inc., 2005.

———, ed. *The Manhattan Project: The Birth of the Atomic Bomb in the Words of Its Creators, Eyewitnesses, and Historians.* Intro by Richard Rhodes. New York: Black Dog & Leventhal Publishers, Inc., 2007.

Klemperer, Victor. *I Will Bear Witness: A Diary of the Nazi Years 1933–1941.* Trans. and with a Preface and Notes by Martin Chalmers. New York: The Modern Library, 1999.

Kreitzer, Carson. *The Love Song of J. Robert Oppenheimer.* Woodstock, IL: Dramatic Publishing, 2006. A play.

Lehman, John. "T. S. Eliot Talks about Himself and the Drive to Create." *The New York Times,* November 9, 1953.

Levi, Primo. *Survival in Auschwitz.* Trans. Stuart Woolf. Miami, FL: BN Publishing, 2007.

Libby, Leona Marshall. *The Uranium People.* New York: Crane, Russak & Company, 1979.

Manchester, William. *The Glory and the Dream: Narrative History of America, 1932–1972.* New York: Little Brown and Co., 1974.

McMillan, Priscilla. *The Ruin of J. Robert Oppenheimer: And the Birth of the Modern Arms Race.* New York: Penguin Books, 2006.

Major, John. *The Oppenheimer Hearing.* New York: Stein and Day, 1971.

Monk, Ray. *Robert Oppenheimer: A Life Inside the Center.* New York: Doubleday, 2012.

Nagel, Ernest, and James R. Newman. *Gödel's Proof.* Revised edition. Edited and with a new Foreword by Douglas R. Hofstadter. New York and London: New York University Press, 2001.

Nelson, Craig. *The Age of Radiance: The Epic Rise and Dramatic Fall of the Atomic Era.* New York: Scribner, 2014.

Oppenheimer. Written by Peter Prince, produced by Peter Goodchild, directed by Barry Davis. Sam Waterston, actor. Studio: BBC Worldwide. Box set, Color, Subtitled, Widescreen, NTSC. 420 minutes; 7 episodes. DVD Release Date: 2008.

Oppenheimer, Robert. *J. Robert Oppenheimer: Letters and Recollections.* Edited by Alice Kimball Smith and Charles Weiner. Cambridge, MA: Harvard University Press, 1980.

———. *Atom and Void: Essays on Science and Community.* Preface by Freeman J. Dyson. Princeton, NJ: Princeton University Press, 1989.

———. *The Flying Trapeze: Three Crises for Physicists.* New York, Harper & Row, 1969.
———. "On Albert Einstein." *The New York Review of Books,* March 17, 1966.
———. *The Open Mind.* New York: Simon and Schuster, 1955.
———. *Science and the Common Understanding.* New York: Simon and Schuster, 1954.

Pais, Abraham. *J. Robert Oppenheimer: A Life.* Robert P. Crease, contributor. New York: Oxford University Press, 2006.

Peirce, Charles S. *Chance, Love, and Logic: Philosophical Essays.* With an intro. by Morris R. Cohen. With a supplementary essay on the pragmatism of Peirce by John Dewey. New York: Barnes & Noble, 1968.

Porter, Jeff. *Oppenheimer Is Watching Me: A Memoir.* Iowa City: University of Iowa Press, 2007.

Raphael, Frederic. *J. Robert Oppenheimer, For Example.* New York: emBooks, 2013. Kindle.

Rhodes, Richard. *The Making of the Atomic Bomb.* Foreword to the 25th Anniversary Edition by author. New York: Simon & Schuster, 1986, 2012.

Ross, Alex. "Countdown." *The New Yorker,* Oct. 3, 2005.

Russell, Bertrand. *Introduction to Mathematical Philosophy.* New York: Macmillan Company, 1924. First published: London: G. Allen & Unwin, Ltd., 1919.

Schell, Jonathan. *The Fate of the Earth.* New York: Alfred A. Knopf, 1982.

Schweber, Silvan S. *Einstein and Oppenheimer: The Meaning of Genius.* Harvard University Press, 2008.

Seabrook, William Todd. *The Genius of J. Robert Oppenheimer.* Newtown, CT: Firewheel Press, 2012. Flash fiction.

Serber, Robert. *The Los Alamos Primer: The First Lectures on How to Build an Atomic Bomb.* Annotated by Serber. Edited and with an Intro. by Richard Rhodes. Berkeley and London: University of California Press, 1992.

See It Now. Interview with J. Robert Oppenheimer. Host, Edward R. Murrow. Producers, Fred W. Friendly and Edward R. Murrow, CBS. January, 1955.

Snow, C. P. *The Physicists.* Intro. by William Cooper. With appendices. Boston, MA: Little, Brown and Co., 1981.
———. *The Search.* Cornwall, UK: House of Stratus, 1958. Novel.
———. *The Two Cultures.* Intro. by Stefan Collini. New York: Cambridge University Press, 1998. With "The Two Cultures: A Second Look (1963)" and Notes by C. P Snow.

Snyder, Sharon, Toni Michnovicz, and the Los Alamos Historical Society. *Los Alamos and the Pajarito Plateau.* Images of America Series. Charleston, NC: Arcadia Publishing, 2011.

Szilard, Leo. *The Voice of the Dolphins and Other Stories.* Intro. and notes by Barton J. Bernstein. Afterword by Helen Weiss. In the Stanford Nuclear Age Series, general ed. Martin J. Sherwin. CA: Stanford University Press, 1961, 1992.

The Day after Trinity. Written, directed, and produced by John Else. With J. Robert Oppenheimer (archive), Hans Bethe, Holm Bursom, Freeman Dyson, Dorothy McKibben, I. I. Rabi, Robert Serber, Robert Wilson, Stanislaw Ulam et al. DVD. Color, NTSC. 88 min. 1980 production date. DVD Release date: May 14, 2002.

The Trials of J. Robert Oppenheimer by David Grubin. Produced and directed by David Grubin. Actors: David Strathairn, Michael Cumpsty. WGBH Boston (American Experience) and PBS DVD. Color and black-and-white. 120 mins. Release date: 2009.

Trinity and Beyond: The Atomic Bomb Movie: Special Edition. Narrated by William Shatner. Special effects filmmaker Peter Kuran. Includes interview with Edward Teller. DVD release date: 1995. Color. 93 mins. A 2006 release runs to 2 discs and includes an interview with Donald Hornig.

Valiunas, Algis. "The Agony of Atomic Genius." *The New Atlantis,* No. 14, Fall 2006, pp. 85–104.

Warner, Edith. *In the Shadow of Los Alamos: Selected Writings of Edith Warner.* Expanded edition. Ed. Patrick Burns, with Preface, Intro., and Appendix. Albuquerque: University of New Mexico Press, 2001.

Weiner, Phillip P. *Values in a Universe of Chance: Selected Writings of Charles S. Peirce.* New York: Dover Publications, 1958.

Wiesel, Elie. *Night.* Foreword by Francois Mauriac. Trans. from the French by Stella Rodway. New York: Hill and Wang, 1960.

Wilson, Jane S., and Charlotte Serber, eds. *Standing By and Making Do: Women of Wartime Los Alamos.* Los Alamos, NM: Los Alamos Historical Society, 2008. 2nd edition.

Wolverton, Mark. *A Life in Twilight: The Final Years of J. Robert Oppenheimer.* New York: St. Martin's Press, 2008.